The 101 Greatest Weapons of All Times

101 GREAT TANKS

Edited by
Robert Jackson

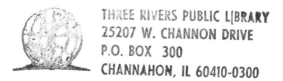

ROSEN
PUBLISHING®
New York

This edition first published in 2010 by:

The Rosen Publishing Group, Inc.
29 East 21st Street
New York, NY 10010

Project Editor: Sarah Uttridge
Picture Research: Terry Forshaw and Kate Green
Design: Graham Curd

Library of Congress Cataloging-in-Publication Data

Jackson, Robert, 1941–
101 great tanks / Robert Jackson, editor.
   p. cm.—(The 101 greatest weapons of all times)
Includes index.
ISBN 978-1-4358-3595-5 (library binding)
1. Tanks (Military science)—History—Juvenile literature. 2. Armored vehicles, Military—History—Juvenile literature. I. Title. II. Title: One hundred one great tanks. III. Title: One hundred and one great tanks.
UG446.5.J234 2010
623.7'4752—dc22

3 1561 00240 7736

2009032880

Manufactured in Malaysia

CPSIA Compliance Information: Batch #TWW10YA: For Further Information contact Rosen Publishing, New York, New York at 1-800-237-9932

Picture credits:
All photographs courtesy of **Art-Tech/Aerospace** except for the following:
Art-Tech/MARS: 8, 61, 6; **BAE Systems:** 5, 108; **Cody Images:** 16, 21, 22, 32, 39, 40, 41, 43, 46, 47, 64, 72, 73, 83, 96, 98, 101; **Christopher Foss:** 105; **Richard Stickland:** 99; **The Tank Museum:** 15, 18, 75; **U.S. Department of Defense:** 6, 77, 91.

All artworks courtesy of **Art-Tech/Aerospace** except for the following:
Alcaniz Fresno's S.A.: 18, 19, 22, 91; **Amber Books:** 13, 17, 21, 26, 30, 35, 41, 43, 44, 49, 55, 65, 69, 76, 78, 79, 80, 82, 86, 87, 88, 90, 94-99, 102, 104, 107; **Ray Hutchins:** 89, 91, 103, 105, 106, 108

Contents

Introduction

Although all the combatant armies relied heavily on horses at the beginning of World War I, the benefits of using armored vehicles to provide mobility, firepower and protection were evident from the first days of the conflict. The British Admiralty was soon pressing commercial motor cars such as the Lanchester and Rolls-Royce into service as armored cars.

But even armored cars could not operate effectively against entrenched and well-defended positions, and the stalemate of the Western Front gave impetus to the development of armored fighting vehicles. It was realized that a new form of mobile strike force was needed. The "tank," as it was code-named for security, was to break the deadlock. Well armored and bristling with weapons, the idea was to cross trenches using the long tracks of the early vehicles and destroy enemy resistance with impunity. The idea was sound enough, and when they first appeared at

the Battle of the Somme in 1916 they proved effective in frightening German conscripts, if not in fulfilling their intended role. Early models were highly unreliable and the tactics employed – using tanks individually to support infantry attacks – were ineffective. However, by the time of the Battle of Cambrai in 1917, improvements had been made. German efforts to catch up with the Allies proved unsuccessful, and by the end of the war tanks were only being produced and used in considerable quantities by the Allies.

If Germany lagged behind the Allies in armored warfare at the end of World War I, during the interwar period they developed a tank arm that was to have a huge impact on warfare. It was not the quality of the armored vehicles but the way in which they were used that proved the value of the armored fighting vehicle. Whereas the French, and the British to some extent, used their armor in small units in an

Although Britain's Challenger 2 main battle tank closely resembles the earlier Challenger 1, it is in fact an entirely new vehicle.

infantry support role, the German Army believed in the value of massed armored formations.

With the development of the superb Panzer V Panther, designed in response to the Russian T-34, and then also the Tiger and King Tiger tanks, the Germans maintained a slight armored advantage throughout the war. However, no matter how powerful and how invulnerable a vehicle was, if it was not mechanically reliable and not available in numbers, its value was limited.

Left: The M1 Abrams main battle tank proved its worth in the Gulf War of 1991, when it tore apart Iraq's Russian-built armor.

Below: Germany's Leopard 2 is an extremely powerful tank and is one of the finest of its generation.

With the complexities of modern tanks, such as the Leclerc, the M1 Abrams and the Challenger, crews must be ever more expert and ever more specialist. The danger of throwing inadequately trained crews in inferior equipment into battle against such specialists in the best vehicles available was fully illustrated in the 1991 Gulf War. There the Iraqi armored divisions were decimated by the Coalition forces who suffered practically no casualties themselves, a scenario largely repeated during the 2003 invasion of Iraq.

The vehicles included in this book are the most influential and important fighting machines in land warfare since World War I. The entries are in chronological order, enabling the reader to witness the ongoing evolution of armored warfare through the decades.

Little Willie

Designed and built on the initiative of the British Admiralty, and in particular Winston Churchill, Little Willie was the world's first practical armored fighting vehicle, rudimentary though it was.

COUNTRY OF ORIGIN: United Kingdom

CREW: 3

WEIGHT: 40,400 lb (18,300 kg)

DIMENSIONS: length: 26.48 ft (8.07 m); width: 11.38 ft (3.47 m); height: 11 ft (3.2 m)

ARMOR: (mild steel) 0.23 in (6 mm)

ARMAMENT: none

POWERPLANT: one x Daimler 6-cylinder petrol, developing 105 hp (78.29 kW) at 100 rpm

PERFORMANCE: maximum road speed 2 mph (3.2 km/h)

For security reasons, Britain's first armored vehicle was known as a tank. The name became firmly established in military parlance.

Little Willie can lay claim to being the progenitor of all armored fighting vehicles. In 1915, two British Army officers, Colonel Ernest Swinton and Colonel Maurice Hankey, convinced Winston Churchill, then First Lord of the Admiralty, that petrol-driven tractors armored with steel plates could cross enemy trenches while remaining impervious to small-arms fire. They were called tanks because they resembled water tanks.

Disappointing performance

Little Willie appeared in prototype form in September 1915, but its performance was disappointing. Its Daimler six-cylinder engine could only power the 17.7 ton (17,984 kg) vehicle at 2 mph (3.2 km/h) on rough ground. It was also unable to traverse significant trenches,

but nonetheless, Little Willie began the race for armored development. It may seem strange that it was the British Admiralty, not the War Office, that proposed the setting up of a Landships Committee to investigate the feasibility of developing a machine, originally intended to be a troop transporter, that would cross deep and wide and be able to suppress enemy weapons, but the Admiralty was responsible for many innovative ideas in World War I, including the development of the long-range strategic bomber.

The choice of the name "tank" to disguise Little Willie's true function was dictated by its appearance, which is evident in this illustration.

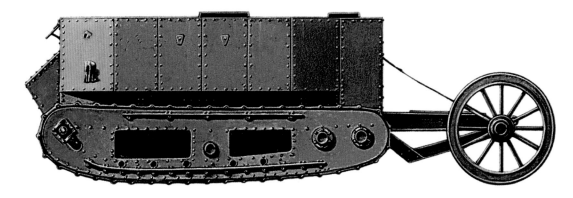

Char d'Assaut St Chamond

The Char d'Assaut St Chamond, although classed as a tank, was in fact the ancestor of all future self-propelled guns. It saw action during most of World War I.

COUNTRY OF ORIGIN: France	
CREW: 9	
WEIGHT: 51,480 lb (23,400 kg)	
DIMENSIONS: length with gun 28 ft 11.75 in (8.83 m); length of hull 25 ft 11.5 in (7.91 m); width 8 ft 9 in (2.67 m); height 7 ft 5.66 in (2.34 m)	
RANGE: 36.7 miles (59 km)	
ARMOR: 0.67 in (17 mm)	
ARMAMENT: one Modèle 1897 2.95 in (75 mm) gun; up to four machine guns	
POWERPLANT: one 90 hp (67 kW) Panhard four-cylinder petrol engine powering a Crochat-Collardeau electric transmission	
PERFORMANCE: maximum road speed 5.3 mph (8.5 km/h)	

The Char d'Assaut St Chamond's design made it a far from ideal vehicle for operations on anything other than level terrain.

The St Chamond was the French Army's own development. The first prototype appeared in 1916. Its poor cross-country performance restricted its use in action, its last major action being a counterattack near Reims in July 1918. Many were converted into Char de Ravitaillement supply carriers and were used in this new role in the final days of World War I.

Limited tactical usefulness

Like the Schneider, the St Chamond was based on the Holt tractor. It had an unusual petrol engine-driven electric transmission, which added an extra five tons (5.1 tonnes) to the design weight. The hull extended both forward and rear of the track which, when combined with the weight, caused the St Chamond to become stuck on rough ground or over trenches. Another serious problem suffered by the vehicle was that the length of the hull greatly restricted the traverse of the main armament, which made the vehicle of very limited tactical usefulness. Nevertheless, it was employed with some effect from April 1915 until the end of World War I, and was the forerunner of all types of self-propelled gun in use to the present day. The AFV was designed by Colonel Rimailho and built at the Saint Chamond factory, Homecourt. By the end of the war, only 72 out of 400 that were produced were still in service.

The length of the St Chamond, combined with its bulk, made the vehicle unwieldy and difficult to handle in some conditions.

Char d'Assaut Schneider

The Schneider Char d'Assaut was France's first true tank, as distinct from a self-propelled gun, but it had many defects and suffered serious losses in combat, mainly when engaged by artillery.

Schneider tanks moving up to the front near L'Eglantiers on the Oise. The crew are perched on top to escape the heat of the engine.

COUNTRY OF ORIGIN: France

CREW: 7

WEIGHT: 32,560 lb (14,800 kg)

DIMENSIONS: length 19 ft 8 in (6.0 m); width 6 ft 6.66 in (2.0 m); height 7 ft 10 in (2.39 m)

RANGE: 30 miles (48 km)

ARMOR: 0.45 in (11.5 mm)

ARMAMENT: one 2.95 in (75 mm) gun, two additional machine guns

POWERPLANT: one 55 hp (41 kW) Schneider four-cylinder petrol engine

PERFORMANCE: maximum road speed 3.7 mph (6 km/h)

The Char d'Assaut Schneider was developed as an armored tractor for towing armored troop sledges across to the German trenches on the Western Front. Based on the American Holt agricultural tractor, the first were available in the middle of 1917. The Schneider Char d'Assaut was the brainchild of Colonel J.E. Estienne, who had made an in-depth study of the American Holt tractor's track and chassis system. In January 1915 Schneider's chief designer, Eugene Brillié, went to the USA to study the Holt tractors for himself, and as a result came back with a proposal for a Tracteur Blindé et Armé (armored and armed tractor).

Difficulty crossing obstacles

The petrol tanks were vulnerable to enemy fire and burned easily. Used mainly for infantry support rather than as personnel carriers, they were restricted by poor cross-country mobility, mainly due to their short tracks and long body, which hindered the vehicle when crossing obstacles. The gun version ceased production in May 1917, to be replaced by the Char de Ravitaillement variant, used for carrying stores. Attrition and poor reliability led to fewer than 100 being in service at the end of the war.

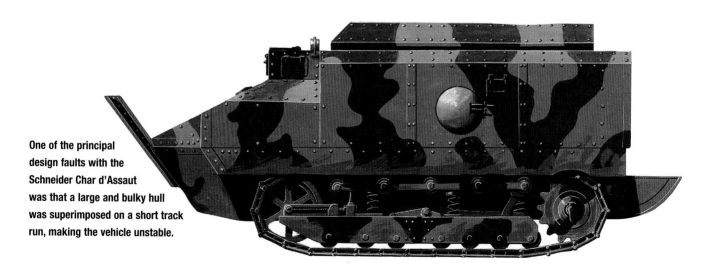

One of the principal design faults with the Schneider Char d'Assaut was that a large and bulky hull was superimposed on a short track run, making the vehicle unstable.

Renault FT-17

The Renault FT-17 was arguably the finest tank of its era and continued in service for many years after the war. Some countries were still using it as a front-line tank in 1939.

COUNTRY OF ORIGIN: France

CREW: 2

WEIGHT: 14,520 lb (6600 kg)

DIMENSIONS: length with tail 16 ft 5 in (5.0 m); width 5 ft 7.33 in (1.71 m); height 7 ft (2.133 m)

RANGE: 22 miles (35.4 km)

ARMOR: 0.63 in (16 mm)

ARMAMENT: one 1.46 in (37 mm) gun or one machine gun

POWERPLANT: one 35 hp (26 kW) Renault four-cylinder petrol engine

PERFORMANCE: maximum road speed 4.8 mph (7.7 km/h)

The FT-17 was a trim little tank. This version has a cast, rather than a riveted, turret. Maintenance was a constant source of concern.

The FT-17 was one of the most successful of all World War I tanks. It was the first of the classic tank design with features mounted directly onto the hull and a turret with a 360-degree traverse. They were ordered in large numbers (more than 3000 during World War I) and needed to be, because they had been designed with little thought for maintenance and repair and as a result were often out of action. A self-propelled gun version and a radio-equipped version were among variants produced. In action, they were used en masse. In one counterattack alone, near Soissons, 480 were used. They remained in service right up until 1944, when the Germans used captured FT-17s for street-fighting in Paris. By this time they were hopelessly out of date.

Impact of future tank design

The FT-17 light tank had a huge impact on future tank design, with its rotating turret mounted on top of the hull and a rear-mounted engine. Because of the French War Department's enthusiasm for super-heavy tanks, the FT-17 might never have been produced had it not been for the continuing support of Colonel Jean-Baptiste Eugène Estienne, who persuaded key figures in the French military that a light infantry support tank would be a valuable tool.

The FT-17 was also used by the US Expeditionary Force in France from the summer of 1918, and the type continued to serve in substantial numbers for years after the war.

Medium Mark A (Whippet)

The Whippet played a vital part in the fighting retreat of the British Army during the German offensive of 1918. Unlike previous British tank designs, this tank was fitted with a revolving turret.

COUNTRY OF ORIGIN: United Kingdom	
CREW: 3 or 4	
WEIGHT: 31,460 lb (14,300 kg)	
DIMENSIONS: length 20 ft (6.10 m); width 8 ft 7 in (2.62 m); height 9 ft (2.74 m)	
RANGE: 160 miles (257 km)	
ARMOR: 0.2–.55 in (5–14 mm)	
ARMAMENT: two Hotchkiss machine guns	
POWERPLANT: two 45 hp (33.6 kW) Tylor four-cylinder petrol engines	
PERFORMANCE: maximum road speed 8.3 mph (13.4 km/h)	

The World War I Medium Tank Mk A light tank was designed not so much for crossing obstacles as for exploiting breakthroughs brought about by heavier tanks. The emphasis was thus on speed and mobility. Designed by William Tritton, the Mk A (nicknamed "Whippet") prototype was powered by London bus engines and was ready in February 1917, but it was not until late 1917 that the first production models appeared.

Proving its value

The Whippet first saw combat in March 1918, plugging gaps in the line. Seven Whippets took part in the second tank-v-tank engagement at Villers Bretonneux/Cachy in April 1918, which took place a few minutes before British Mk IVs engaged German A7Vs. Here, one Whippet was destroyed and another damaged by a German A7V, but the surviving tanks caught two German infantry battalions out in the open and inflicted 400 casualties. Its value was proved in counterattacks, making deep forays behind the lines and creating havoc in the German rear areas. After the war, the Mk A saw service in Ireland and a number were exported to Japan in the 1920s.

This view of the Whippet shows the complex nature of the vehicle's turret superstructure and the large mud chutes under the track tops.

The Whippet seen here carries large red and white identification markings as an insurance against being engaged by friendly fire. The vehicle's main task was to exploit a breakthrough into enemy territory.

A7V Sturmpanzerwagen

Used to good effect in the Ludendorff offensive of March 1918, the A7V was Germany's first viable tank. It also fought the first-ever tank-versus-tank battle.

After the war a few A7Vs were taken over by the newly formed Polish Army, and some were used in Germany's internal struggles.

COUNTRY OF ORIGIN: Germany	
CREW: 18	
WEIGHT: 73,700 lb (33,500 kg)	
DIMENSIONS: length 26 ft 3 in (8.0 m); width 10 ft 0.5 in (3.06 m); height 10 ft 10 in (3.30 m)	
RANGE: 25 miles (40 km)	
ARMOR: 0.39–1.18 in (10–30 mm)	
ARMAMENT: one 2.24 in (57 mm) gun; six machine guns	
POWERPLANT: two 100 hp (74.6 kW) Daimler petrol engines	
PERFORMANCE: maximum road speed 8 mph (12.9 km/h)	

The Sturmpanzerwagen A7V was an enormous vehicle, hurriedly designed following the appearance of British tanks in 1916. The Germans gave the development of armored fighting vehicles much lower priority than did both the British and French. By 1917 the Germans were on the defensive, and it was argued that tanks, as offensive weapons, had no place in defensive strategy. A special committee, called the A7V Committee for security reasons, was formed in October 1917 to study the concept of the armored fighting vehicle, and by the end of the year it had designed a machine based on the Holt suspension. Ground clearance was only 1.57 in (40 mm) and the length of track on the ground was too short for a vehicle of its size. The result was an unstable vehicle with poor cross-country performance.

Lagging behind the infantry

100 A7Vs were ordered in December 1917, but the German war machine was already stretched and only about 20 were ever produced. Their shortcomings over rough ground were manifested in March 1918 when they first saw action, and they often lagged behind the infantry they were designed to support. Variants included the Überlandwagen, an open-topped, unarmored supply version, and the A7V/U with "all-round" tracks. Post-war, they were used by the Polish Army for some years.

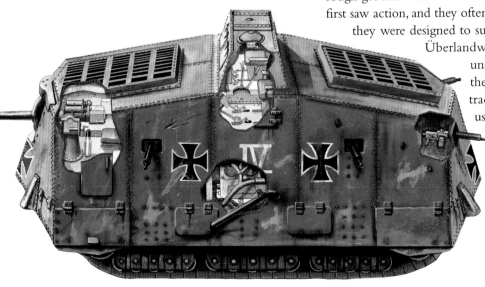

The A7V was Germany's first successful tank design. It took part in the world's first tank-versus-tank battle.

Tank Mk V

About 400 Mk Vs had been built in Birmingham by the time of the Armistice in November 1918, and by then several variants were being manufactured.

COUNTRY OF ORIGIN:	United Kingdom
CREW:	8
WEIGHT:	65,120 lb (29,600 kg)
DIMENSIONS:	length 26 ft 5 in (8.05 m); width over sponsons 13 ft 6 in (4.11 m); height 8 ft 8 in (2.64 m)
RANGE:	45 miles (72 km)
ARMOR:	0.24–0.55 in (6–14 mm)
ARMAMENT:	two 6-pounder guns, four Hotchkiss machine guns
POWERPLANT:	one 150 hp (112 kW) Ricardo petrol engine
PERFORMANCE:	maximum road speed 4.6 mph (7.4 km/h)

This Mk V carries red and white recognition markings. The rails over the top of the hull are for "unditching" beams.

The Tank Mk V was the last of the lozenge-shaped tanks to see service in any number. It was designed to take part in the massive armored thrusts envisaged for 1919. Improvements on earlier models included a Wilson epicyclic gearbox, which allowed the tank to be driven by one man as opposed to two in earlier models. There was a cupola for the commander. Semaphore arms were mounted to give effective communication for the first time. The Tank Mk V★ variant had a new 6 ft (1.83 m) section in the hull to improve trench-crossing capability and provide extra internal space. From mid-1918, the tank saw action with the British and Americans. Post-war variants included bridge-laying and mine-clearing versions, and it remained in service with the Canadians until the early 1930s.

Arrival in 1918

The Mk V arrived on the Western Front from about mid-1918 onwards. It proved to be more reliable and easier to handle than earlier marks, but the war ended before it had a chance to prove itself in the operations that were being planned for 1918. These missions called for the massed deployment of Mk Vs, along with some special tanks that never left the drawing board.

An innovation introduced in the Mk V was a cupola for the commander, and the mounting of semaphore arms on the back of the hull for communication with other tanks or infantry.

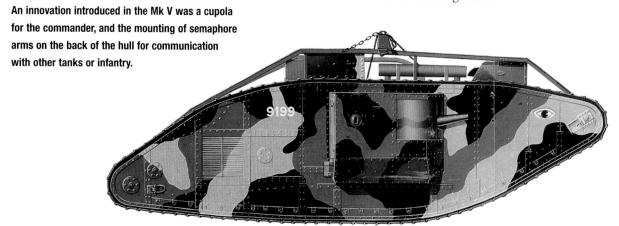

Carden-Loyd Mk VI Tankette

A cross between a light tank and a machine-gun carrier, the Carden-Loyd Tankette was a huge success on the export market, being cheap to purchase and reproduce.

COUNTRY OF ORIGIN: United Kingdom	
CREW: 2	
WEIGHT: 3500 lb (1600 kg)	
DIMENSIONS: length 8.1 ft (2.47 m); width 5.58 ft (1.7 m); height 4 ft (1.22 m)	
RANGE: 100 miles (160 km)	
ARMOR: 0.35 in (9 mm) maximum	
ARMAMENT: one x 0.303 in (7.7 mm) Vickers MG	
POWERPLANT: one x Ford T 4-cylinder petrol, developing 40 hp (30kW)	
PERFORMANCE: maximum road speed: 28 mph (45 km/h)	

The whole purpose of the Carden-Loyd Mk VI was to permit the rapid deployment of infantry in protected conditions under fire.

Carden-Loyd tankettes were an unsuccessful interwar experiment in providing armored mobile machine-gun carriers for pairs of infantrymen. The first tankette was produced in 1925, a small tracked vehicle big enough for one man only, subsequently topped with a flimsy shield and a Hotchkiss machine gun to form the Carden-Loyd Mk I. Several variations were then produced, focusing mainly on experiments with track and suspension configurations. In 1926, a two-man version was produced which became the Vickers machine-gun-armed Carden-Loyd Mk IV in 1928. Two more versions emerged and achieved some sales abroad, but were tactically impractical and had no future past the mid-1930s. The Mk VI and earlier versions were also used by the British Army, which took delivery of 270.

Rapid deployment of troops

The purpose of the Tankette was the rapid deployment of troops armed with machine guns, which were not intended to be fired from the vehicle itself, although a tripod mounting for a machine gun was attached to the front of the hull. Tankettes could also tow light howitzers.

Although the Carden-Loyd Mk VI initially failed its trials with the British Army, 270 examples were eventually purchased for use as artillery tractors.

Renault UE Chenillette

A very versatile utility vehicle, the little Renault UE Chenillette was widely used throughout the world in support of France's colonial interests. Many were used by the Germans. Its design owed much to the Carden-Loyd vehicles.

The Renault UE Chenillette was widely used by the French colonial forces in their various "police" actions.

COUNTRY OF ORIGIN: France	
CREW: 2	
WEIGHT: 7300 lb (3300 kg)	
DIMENSIONS: length 9.64 ft (2.94 m); width 5.74 ft (1.75 m); height 4.07 ft (1.24 m)	
RANGE: 80 miles (125 km)	
ARMOR: not available	
ARMAMENT: none	
POWERPLANT: one Renault 85 4-cylinder petrol, developing 38 hp (28kW)	
PERFORMANCE: maximum road speed: 30 mph (48 km/h)	

The Renault UE or "Universal Carrier" was indebted in design to the British Carden-Loyd tankettes developed between the wars. With a two-man crew and a 38 hp (28 kW) Renault 85 engine, it could pull 1300 lb (600 kg) or carry 775 lb (350 kg) of materials in its rear storage compartment and travel at 30 mph (48 km/h), powered by a Renault 85 four-cylinder petrol engine. Each crew member had a rounded dome cover for overhead protection. Following the 1940 German occupation of France, the Germans pressed the Renault UE into service for ammunition carriage or for airfield security patrols.

As an infantry support vehicle in German service, the UE could be armed with one or two MG34 machine guns.

Widely used by the French

The UE was widely used by the French in Indochina, and in the late 1930s represented the only effective armored vehicles available to the French colonial forces, because most of the light tanks that had been deployed there at earlier dates were no longer roadworthy. The UEs were formed into motorized detachments.

The Renault UE was the approximate equivalent of Britain's Bren-Gun Carrier and fulfilled much the same purpose. It served in large numbers.

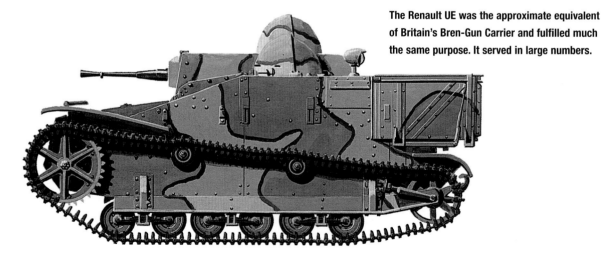

Type 95 Light Tank

The Type 95 Ha-Go was the first light tank of Japanese design to go into full production, and saw service in China and the Pacific, enjoying a good deal of success in the early months.

COUNTRY OF ORIGIN: Japan	
CREW: 4	
WEIGHT: 16,280 lb (7400 kg)	
DIMENSIONS: length 14 ft 4 in (4.38 m); width 6 ft 9 in (2.057 m); height 7 ft 2 in (2.184 m)	
RANGE: 156 miles (250 km)	
ARMOR: 0.25–0.6 in (6–14 mm)	
ARMAMENT: one 1.46 in (37 mm) gun; two 0.303 in (7.7 mm) machine guns	
POWERPLANT: one Mitsubishi NVD 6120 six-cylinder air-cooled diesel engine developing 120 hp (89 kW)	
PERFORMANCE: maximum road speed 28 mph (45 km/h); fording 3 ft 3 in (1.0 m); vertical obstacle 2 ft 8 in (0.812m); trench 6 ft 7 in (2.0 m)	

The Type 95 was one of the first Japanese tanks to enter production.

The Type 95, known as the Ha-Go, was developed in the early 1930s for the Japanese Army. When production ceased in 1943, over 1100 had been built. The major drawback of the vehicle was that the commander had to operate the gun in addition to his normal duties, which impeded combat effectiveness. While this was acceptable when faced with infantry in Manchuria, it proved disastrous when up against US armor in the later years of the war. Despite later upgunning, the tank's poor armor and lack of firepower ensured that it was wholly inadequate. The Type 95 also served as the basis for the Type 2 KA-MI amphibious tank widely used in early Pacific campaigns of World War II.

Vulnerable to anti-armor weaponry

It was followed by an improved version, the Light Tank Type 98, which entered service in 1942. The light tanks were used with some success in the early Pacific campaigns, especially against Allied infantry unsupported by tanks of their own, and were also used in a defensive role with Japanese garrisons on the Pacific islands, notably Tarawa Atoll. They proved extremely vulnerable to Allied anti-armor weapons such as the Bazooka.

The Type 95 was derived from the Type 89, which entered limited production and which was in turn derived from the Vickers Mk C.

BT-7

Russia's BT-7 light tank was used in large numbers and saw considerable action in border skirmishes between the USSR and Japan, but it was obsolete by the summer of 1941.

The BT-7 was the ultimate Soviet development of vehicles designed by J. Walter Christie and incorporated numerous improvements.

COUNTRY OF ORIGIN: USSR	
CREW: 3	
WEIGHT: 13.83 tons (14.050 kg)	
DIMENSIONS: length 18 ft 8 in (5.68 m); width 7ft (2.43 m); height 7 ft 6 in (2.28 m)	
RANGE: 155 miles (250 km)	
ARMOR: 0.236–0.866 in (6–22 mm)	
ARMAMENT: one 1.77 in (45 mm) M-32 gun, two 0.3 in (7.62 mm) DT MGs	
POWERPLANT: M-17T 12-cylinder petrol, 335.8 kW (450b hp) at 1750 rpm	
PERFORMANCE: maximum speed 53.4 mph (86 km/h); fording 3 ft 11 in (1.2 m); vertical obstacle 2 ft 6 in (0.75 m); trench 6 ft 7 in (2 m)	

The Soviet BT-7 light tank of 1935 was a logical development of the BT-5, incorporating various refinements as a result of the lessons learned during border conflicts in the Far East in the early 1930s. Fast and agile, the BT-7 was very popular with its crews, particularly because it was mechanically sound and simple to maintain. Both BT-5s and BT-7s were used in further border skirmishes with the Japanese in 1939, and were found to be superior to Japanese AFVs in their class. The BT-7 was the principal Soviet tank used in the occupation of eastern

Poland in 1939, and large numbers were used in action against the invading Germans in 1941, suffering fearsome losses. Most of the surviving BT tanks were shipped to the Far East, where they were employed in the Soviet invasion of Manchuria in 1945.

Less armor, more speed

Several versions of the BT-7 were built, including a close support variant armed with a 3 in (76 mm) main gun. The BT-7 could be fitted with tracks of varying width for use on different types of terrain. In action, the BT-7's biggest drawback was its lack of armor, sacrificed to achieve speed.

Some BT tanks were tested under operational conditions during the Spanish Civil War and were used in the "Winter War" against Finland.

T-26

Russia's T-26 tank saw widespread service in the years between the wars and provided Soviet Army tank men with much-needed experience, enabling them to develop better tactics.

COUNTRY OF ORIGIN: USSR	
CREW: 3	
WEIGHT: 10.3 tons (10,460 kg)	
DIMENSIONS: length 15 ft 9 in (4.8 m); width: 7 ft 10 in (2.39 m); height 7 ft 8 in (2.33 m)	
RANGE: 124 miles (200 km)	
ARMOR: 0.39–0.98 in (10–25 mm)	
ARMAMENT: one 1.77 in (45 mm) Model 1938 L/46 gun; two 0.3 in (7.62 mm) DT MGs	
POWERPLANT: GAZ T-26 8-cylinder petrol. 67.9 kW (91b hp) at 2200 rpm	
PERFORMANCE: maximum speed 17.4 mph (28 km/h); fording not known; vertical obstacle 2 ft 7 in (0.79 m); trench 6 ft 3 in (1.9 m)	

Later models of the T-26 were fitted with a single turret, in which guise the vehicle was designated T-26B.

The T-26, a mass-produced version of the British Vickers Type E 6-ton (6,096 kg) tank, was an extremely important milestone in the development of the Soviet Union's armored forces. Not only did it provide a substantial nucleus of Russian tank men with practical experience of operating what was then a modern armored fighting vehicle, but it also led directly to many improvements that would be incorporated in later generations of Soviet AFVs, placing them among the finest in the world. The initial models of the T-26, the T-26A series, had twin turrets each mounting a machine gun (or, later, one machine gun and one cannon), but this configuration was soon abandoned in favor of the more practical single turret, in which guise the AFV became the T-26B. This saw service in large numbers from 1933, around 5500 being produced before production ended in 1936. The T-26B was followed by the T-26S of 1937, which had a turret of improved design and was of all-welded construction.

Pressed into Finnish service

The T-26 was vulnerable to anti-tank weapons, such as the German 1.46 in (37 mm) towed anti-tank gun: during the 1939–40 conflict with Finland, dozens of knocked-out T-26s were captured by the Finns, repaired and pressed into service, most of them still in use at the end of World War II.

The T-26 was supplied in some numbers to the Republican government in the Spanish Civil War, and proved to be greatly superior to Germany's Panzer Mk I.

T-28 Medium Tank

Russia's T-28 was the first operational medium tank in the world and incorporated several innovations, including radio equipment. However, its inadequate armor caused problems in action.

COUNTRY OF ORIGIN: USSR

CREW: 6

WEIGHT: 62,720 lb (28,509 kg)

DIMENSIONS: length 24 ft 4.8 in (7.44 m); width 9 ft 2.75 in (2.81 m); height 9 ft 3 in (2.82 m)

RANGE: 136.7 miles (220 km)

ARMOR: 0.39–3.15 in (10–80 mm)

ARMAMENT: one 3 in (76.2 mm) gun; three 0.30 in (7.62 mm) machine guns

POWERPLANT: one M-17 V-12 petrol engine developing 500 hp (373 kW)

PERFORMANCE: maximum road speed 23 mph (37 km/h); fording not known; vertical obstacle 3 ft 5 in (1.04 m); trench 9 ft 6 in (2.90 m)

Inspired by British and German tank designs, the T-28 medium tank had a centrally mounted main turret and two auxiliary machine-gun turrets in front. The vehicle's suspension was directly copied from the British Vickers vehicle, and though the prototype was armed with a 1.77 in (45 mm) main gun, production models were equipped with the more powerful 3 in (76.2 mm) low-velocity gun. There were a number of different models and variants, some of which were produced as a result of combat experience. The T-28C, for example, was given additional armor on the hull front and turret as a result of the Red Army's unhappy time in the Russo-Finnish War. An interesting variant was the T-28(V), a commander's tank fitted with a radio that had a frame aerial round the turret.

First operational medium tank

Although in many respects Russia's T-28 was a prime example of how a tank should not be designed, it was nevertheless the first operational medium tank in the world, and as such deserves its place in history. Even though some of its design features were influenced by earlier British experimental AFVs, notably the Vickers types, it was of indigenous design and paved the way for future Soviet medium tank developments. The prototype was completed in 1931.

The Soviet T-28 was a clumsy vehicle, with armor that proved much too thin in combat. It was classed as a medium tank, even though it weighed 28 tons (28,449 kg).

The bulky design of the T-28 is apparent in this illustration. It suffered appalling losses during the Winter War of 1939–40, where its inadequate armor was easily penetrated by Finnish anti-tank projectiles.

Panzer I

Because of the Treaty of Versailles, which forbade Germany to manufacture tanks, the Germans had to produce their first post–Word War I tank, the Panzer I, in strict secrecy.

COUNTRY OF ORIGIN: Germany

CREW: 2

WEIGHT: 12,100 lb (5500 kg)

DIMENSIONS: length 13.2 ft (4.02 m); width 6 ft 7 in (2.06 m); height 5 ft 7 in (1.72 m)

RANGE: 81 miles (145 km)

ARMOR: 0.2–0.5 in (6–13 mm)

ARMAMENT: two 0.31 in (7.92 mm) MG13 machine guns

POWERPLANT: one Krupp M305 petrol engine developing 60 hp (45 kW)

PERFORMANCE: maximum road speed 21 mph (37 km/h); fording 2 ft 10 in (0.85 m); vertical obstacle 1 ft 5 in (0.42 m); trench 5 ft 9 in (1.75 m)

The Panzerkampf-wagen I was heavily involved in the Polish campaign, having earlier proved itself in the Spanish Civil War.

The Panzer I was the first German tank to go into mass production, with nearly 600 having been ordered by July 1934. Three separate companies were engaged to build the tank (deliberately to spread experience of tank manufacture as widely as possible) and over 800 had been produced by June 1936, when production ceased. To avoid being seen to break the Treaty of Versailles the design was disguised as an "agricultural tractor." To conceal the true nature of the vehicle, the Henschel Company received an order to build an initial batch of 150 "industrial tractors." By the time production started in July 1934 all pretense of secrecy had been abandoned by the Nazi regime.

Ready for the invasion of Poland

The tanks came off the production line under their correct military designation. The PzKpfw I was evaluated under operational conditions in Spain, and by the time Germany invaded Poland in September 1939 the Wehrmacht had over 1400 on charge.

The campaign in Poland showed that the PzKpfw I was too light and vulnerable to be effective in the front line, but despite this some 500 were used in the French campaign of 1940.

Panzer II Light Tank

The Panzer II, which effectively bridged the gap between the Panzer I and more advanced fighting vehicles, was the vehicle in which German tank crews trained for the campaigns of World War II.

COUNTRY OF ORIGIN: Germany

CREW: 3

WEIGHT: 22,046 lb (10,000 kg)

DIMENSIONS: length 15 ft 3 in (4.64 m); width 7 ft 6.5 in (2.30 m); height 6 ft 7.5 in (2.02 m)

RANGE: 125 miles (200 km)

ARMOR: (Ausf F version) 0.8–1.38 in (20–35 mm)

ARMAMENT: one 0.79 in (20 mm) cannon; one 0.31 in (7.92 mm) machine gun

POWERPLANT: one Maybach six-cylinder petrol engine developing 140 hp (104 kW)

PERFORMANCE: maximum road speed 34 mph (55 km/h); fording 2 ft 10 in (0.85 m); vertical obstacle 1 ft 5 in (0.42 m); trench 5 ft 9 in (1.75 m)

Tactics and radio communications ensured victory of German light tanks like the Panzer II over numerically superior armored forces.

The first production model PzKpfw II Ausf A appeared in 1935, having been designated as a tractor since German rearmament was restricted by the Treaty of Versailles. The initial tanks were a collaboration between the firms of MAN and Daimler-Benz. The Ausf B, C, D, E and F versions were built during the years up to 1941, the main improvements being in the thickness of the armor. The tank formed the backbone of the invasions of Poland and France, with around 1000 seeing service. By the time of the invasion of the USSR in 1941, the tank was obsolete but was the basis for the Luchs reconnaissance tank. Other variants included an amphibious version designed for the invasion of Britain and the Flammpanzer II flame-throwing tank.

A simple solution

The specification called for a 10-ton (10,160 kg) armored vehicle mounting a 0.79 in (20 mm) gun in a fully revolving turret. Krupps proposed a simple solution, involving the mounting of a 0.79 in (20 mm) cannon and machine gun in the existing PzKpfw I, but ultimately it was a vehicle proposed by MAN that was selected for production.

The Panzer II was a very mobile and effective light tank, and like other German fighting vehicles of its time it was tested in action during the civil war in Spain.

Somua S-35 Medium Tank

Without doubt the best medium tank in service in the world in 1940, the SOMUA (Société d'Outillage Mécanique et d'Usinage d'Artillerie) was designed in response to a requirement for a new cavalry tank issued in 1934.

COUNTRY OF ORIGIN: France

CREW: 3

WEIGHT: 42,900 lb (19,500 kg)

DIMENSIONS: length 17 ft 7.8 in (5.38 m); width 6 ft 11.5 in (2.12 m); height 8 ft 7 in (2.62 m)

RANGE: 143 miles (230 km)

ARMOR: 0.8–2.2 in (20–55 mm)

ARMAMENT: one 1.85 in (47 mm) gun; one coaxial 0.30 in (7.5 mm) machine gun

POWERPLANT: one SOMUA V-8 petrol engine developing 190 hp (141.7 kW)

PERFORMANCE: maximum road speed 24.85 mph (40 km/h); fording 3 ft 3 in (1.0 m); vertical obstacle 2 ft 6 in (0.76 m); trench 7 ft (2.13 m)

The SOMUA S-35 was one of the first tanks used to mechanize the French cavalry in the mid-1930s. It was a very advanced vehicle for its time and many of its features were to become standard for future tank designs, such as cast, rather than rivetted, armor. A radio was fitted as standard and the tank was supplied with a sufficiently powerful main armament to be still in service in German hands on D-Day in June 1944. Production was slow and there were only around 250 in front-line service by the time the Germans invaded in 1940. The major drawback was that the commander was required to operate the gun and the radio as well as his normal duties, yet the S-35 was still the best Allied tank available in service in 1940.

Mechanically reliable

In action, the SOMUA could out-pace and out-gun the German Panzer III, but the German tank was much more reliable mechanically, the SOMUA experiencing problems with its complex suspension (designed by Eugène Brillié, the man who had been responsible for the development of France's first tank, the Schneider AC1). The SOMUA acquitted itself well during the Battle of France, being well protected and maneuverable and armed with a gun that could fire both armor-piercing shot and high-explosive shell.

Captured SOMUA S-35 medium tanks are seen taking part in the German victory parade along the Champs-Elysées. after the fall of France.

Well protected and agile, the SOMUA S-35 was the finest tank in the world in 1940, incorporating many novel features that had escaped the attention of other designers.

Renault R-35 Light Tank

The Renault R-35 two-man infantry light tank was built in the erroneous belief that tank warfare had changed little since 1918, and was designed in accordance with the concepts developed in World War I.

The R-35 was obsolete in its concept, and as a result proved inadequate on the battlefield when pitted against the Panzers.

COUNTRY OF ORIGIN: France

CREW: 2

WEIGHT: 22,046 lb (10,000 kg)

DIMENSIONS: length 13 ft 9.25 in (4.20 m); width 6 ft 0.75 in (1.85 m); height 7 ft 9.25 in (2.37 m)

RANGE: 87 miles (140 km)

ARMOR: 1.57 in (40 mm)

ARMAMENT: one 1.46 in (37 mm) gun; one coaxial 0.30 in (7.5 mm) machine gun

POWERPLANT: one Renault four-cylinder petrol engine developing 82 hp (61 kW)

PERFORMANCE: maximum road speed 12.4 mph (20 km/h); fording 2 ft 7 in (0.80 m); vertical obstacle 1 ft 7.7 in (0.50 m); trench 5 ft 3 in (1.60 m)

The Renault R-35 was designed in the mid-1930s to replace the ageing World War I-vintage Renault FT-17. By 1940, some 1600 had been built and it was the most numerous French tank in service, even though it never managed to fulfil its role as the FT-17's replacement. In 1938 the Polish Army subjected two R-35s to a thorough evaluation, and was not impressed. But the Poles were short of tanks, so they placed an order for 100 units, the first 50 of which were delivered in July 1939, only weeks before the German invasion.

Abandoned in retreat

On May 10, 1940, at the start of the Battle of France, R-35s equipped 21 battalions, each of 45 vehicles. It was no match for German panzers, particularly as it was deployed piecemeal against their massed formations. Unable to penetrate even light German armor, many were abandoned during the French retreat in May 1940. The Germans used the R-35 as a garrison and training tank and adapted many for use as artillery tractors, ammunition carriers and self-propelled artillery carriages. For the latter, the turrets were removed and used for coastal defenses.

The Renault R-35 light tank was typical of the fighting vehicles of this era. It was designed to replace the excellent FT-17 in service, but never quite succeeded in doing so.

Vickers Light Tank

The Vickers light tanks were intended primarily to police Britain's extensive colonial possessions, but they proved lacking in capability against German tanks early in World War II.

COUNTRY OF ORIGIN: United Kingdom	
CREW: 3	
WEIGHT: 10,729 lb (4877 kg)	
DIMENSIONS: length 13 ft (3.96 m); width 6 ft 10 in (2.08 m); height 7 ft 6 in (2.235 m)	
RANGE: range 215 miles (201 km)	
ARMOR: 0.4–0.6 in (10–15 mm)	
ARMAMENT: one 0.303 in (7.7 mm)/0.50 in (12.7 mm) machine gun	
POWERPLANT: one Meadows ESTL six-cylinder petrol engine developing 88 hp (66 kW)	
PERFORMANCE: maximum road speed 32 mph (51.5 km/h); fording 2 ft (0.6 m); vertical obstacle 2 ft (0.6 m); trench 5 ft (1.52 m)	

Although poor as infantry support vehicles, the Vickers light tanks were thrown into combat in the Western Desert and had some success.

Originally based on the Carden-Loyd Tankette of the 1920s, the Vickers light tanks were developed in the 1930s. The Carden-Loyd Mk VIII served as the prototype Vickers Light Tank Mark I. This was followed by the Mk 1A, with better armor, and the Mk II, with an improved turret design and modified suspension. The simple hull design had riveted armor. The early Vickers light tanks carried a two-man crew, but in the Mk V the turret was enlarged to accommodate two men, making a crew of three. Mobile and fast, the Vickers was used in the 1930s for policing the British Empire and in early World War II. However, combat experience proved them to be virtually useless. Their thin armor was easily pierced and their machine-gun armament was utterly inadequate on the battlefield.

Disastrous results

Lack of equipment forced the British to use them in combat rather than for reconnaissance, for which they were designed, with disastrous results. Converting them into anti-aircraft tanks failed, but the Germans managed to use some captured vehicles as anti-tank gun carriers.

The early Vickers light tanks suffered from a wholly inadequate armament and suffered serious losses when they were used in the infantry support role, to which they were not suited.

Char B1 Heavy Tank

The Char B1 heavy tank was a good fighting vehicle, but it was unnecessarily complex and had a limited endurance. It was also expensive to produce, which compelled the French Army to reduce its order.

COUNTRY OF ORIGIN: France

CREW: 4

WEIGHT: 69,300 lb (31,500 kg)

DIMENSIONS: length 20 ft 10.8 in (6.37 m); width 8 ft 2.4 in (2.50 m); height 9 ft 1.8 in (2.79 m)

RANGE: 112 miles (180 km)

ARMOR: 0.6–2.6 in (14–65 mm)

ARMAMENT: one 2.95 in (75 mm) gun; one 1.77 in (45 mm) gun

POWERPLANT: one Renault six-cylinder petrol engine developing 307 hp (229 kW)

PERFORMANCE: maximum road speed 17.4 mph (28 km/h); fording not known; vertical obstacle 3 ft 1 in (0.93 m); trench 9 ft (2.74 m)

The Char B1 could cope with any German tank it encountered, but poor tactical handling made it virtually useless in action.

The first B1s appeared in 1937. Despite its World War I appearance, the Char B1 was a powerful tank for the time and carried a range of advanced features, such as self-sealing fuel tanks. But the crew were seated away from each other, which made communication difficult. These crews needed to be highly trained to operate the B1 to full advantage, and such crews were rare in 1940. In addition, the tank's complexities made maintenance difficult and many broke down in combat.

Cumbersome in combat

Those that entered the fray were really too cumbersome for their powerful armament to have much effect. It was not until January 1940 that the French were in a position to begin forming two heavy armored divisions (Divisions Cuirassées), followed by a third in March. The final production model of the Char B was the B1-bis, with a more powerful engine, thicker armor and a revised turret design. The B1 was later described by the German Panzer General Heinz Guderian as the best tank in the field in 1940. The Germans later employed captured Char B1s as training tanks or self-propelled artillery carriages.

The Char B1, which traced its development back as far as 1921 and was somewhat archaic in appearance (which it was not in reality), was an excellent heavy tank.

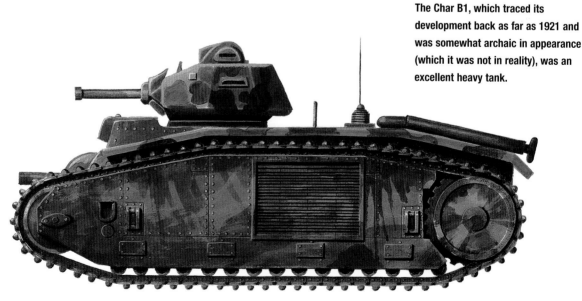

Panzer III Medium Tank

The Panzer III, seen here in desert campaign colors, was numerically the most important German tank. Many were later adapted as self-propelled guns and served throughout the war.

There was nothing to compete with the Panzer III in early World War II, but by the middle of the war it was outclassed by Allied armor.

COUNTRY OF ORIGIN: Germany	
CREW: 5	
WEIGHT: 49,060 lb (22,300 kg)	
DIMENSIONS: length 21 ft (6.41 m); width 9 ft 8 in (2.95 m); height 8 ft 2.5 in (2.50 m)	
RANGE: 110 miles (175 km)	
ARMOR: 1.18 in (30 mm)	
ARMAMENT: (Ausf M version) one 2.95 in (75 mm) L/24 gun; one 0.31 in (7.92 mm) machine gun	
POWERPLANT: one Maybach HL 120 TRM 12-cylinder petrol engine developing 300 hp (224 kW)	
PERFORMANCE: maximum road speed 25 mph (40 km/h); fording 2 ft 8 in (0.8 m); vertical obstacle 2 ft (0.6 m); trench 8 ft 6 in (2.59 m)	

Following a 1935 German Army requirement for a light medium-tank design, in September 1939 Daimler-Benz began mass production of the PzKpfw III. The first three production models, PzKpfw Ausführung A, B and C, were built in relatively small numbers, and these saw action during the invasion of Poland in September 1939. The next model was the Ausf D, which had thicker armor and a revised cupola. In 1940 the Ausf F entered production, armed with a high-velocity 2 in (50 mm) gun and an uprated engine, and fitted with only six road wheels. The Ausf G had a similar armament, but had a more powerful engine. By the time the final version, the Ausf N, ceased production in August 1943, when the army was fighting in Russia, the tank carried twice as big a gun and weighed twice as much as the original prototype.

Numerous variants

Variants included an amphibious version, a command vehicle, an armored recovery vehicle, an observation vehicle and one adapted for desert warfare. In addition, the chassis was used for a number of self-propelled guns right to the end of World War II in 1945.

The Panzer III was without doubt one of the best tanks to be produced during World War II, being made in several versions and used for many different tasks. It was originally designed as a tank destroyer.

Panzer IV Medium Tank

One of the most important armored fighting vehicles of World War II, the PzKpfw IV, commonly referred to as the Panzer IV, was intended for the infantry support role, leaving the Panzer III to deal with enemy armor.

COUNTRY OF ORIGIN: Germany

CREW: 5

WEIGHT: 55,000 lb (25,000 kg)

DIMENSIONS: length 23 ft (7.02 m); width 10 ft 9.5 in (3.29 m); height 8 ft 9.5 in (2.68 m)

RANGE: 125 miles (200 km)

ARMOR: 1.97–2.4 in (50–60 mm)

ARMAMENT: (Ausf H version) one 2.95 in (75 mm) gun; two 0.31 in (7.92 mm) MG 34 machine guns

POWERPLANT: one Maybach HL 120 TRM 12-cylinder petrol engine developing 300 hp (224 kW)

PERFORMANCE: maximum road speed 24 mph (38 km/h); fording 3 ft 3 in (1.0 m); vertical obstacle 2 ft (0.6 m); trench 7 ft 3in (2.20 m)

A Panzer IV in action on the Eastern Front. The vehicle is armed with the long 2.95 in (75 mm) high-velocity gun.

The PzKpfw IV was built under a 1934 requirement from the German Army Weapons Department and was later the backbone of the Wehrmacht's panzer arm. In 1941, following the first encounters between the Panzer IV and the Russian T-34, the Panzer IV Ausf F was equipped with a redesigned turret mounting a more powerful 2.95 in (75 mm) L/43 anti-tank gun. In this guise it became the Panzer IVF2, later renamed the Panzer IVG. This variant became the workhorse of the German armored divisions and remained basically unchanged except for upgrades in its main armament and armor. In production throughout the war, the final version,

Ausf J, appeared in March 1944. In total, Krupp built nearly 9000 vehicles, the basic chassis remaining the same, but with heavier armor and armament added as requirements changed.

Chassis remained the same

Despite the extra weight, the PzKpfw IV retained a good power-to-weight ratio throughout its production life and had good mobility. Like the Panzer III, the chassis was used as the basis for various self-propelled guns as well as armored recovery vehicles and bridge-layers and the Jagdpanzer IV tank destroyer.

This Panzer IV, depicted late in the war, has had extra armor plate added to its hull and turret to protect it against the latest Allied anti-tank projectiles.

PzKpfw 38(t)

Widely used by Germany's allies on the Eastern Front, the PzKpfw 38(t) (LT-38) was yet another demonstration of the excellence of the war material produced by the Czech armaments industry.

COUNTRY OF ORIGIN: Germany
CREW: 4
WEIGHT: 21,340 lb (9700 kg)
DIMENSIONS: length 14 ft 11 in (4.546 m); width 7 ft (2.133 m); height 7 ft 7 in (2.311 m)
RANGE: 125 miles (200 km)
ARMOR: 0.4–1 in (10–25 mm); later increased from Ausf E version onwards to 2 in (50 mm)
ARMAMENT: one 1.46 in (37.2 mm) Skoda A7 gun; two 0.31 in (7.92 mm) machine guns
POWERPLANT: one Praga EPA six-cylinder water-cooled inline petrol engine developing 150 hp (112 kW)
PERFORMANCE: maximum road speed 26 mph (42 km/h); fording 3 ft (0.9 m); vertical obstacle 2 ft 7 in (0.787 m); trench 6 ft 2 in (1.879 m)

A PzKpfw pictured in action during the invasion of France. The 7th and 8th Panzer Divisions used the vehicle during this campaign.

The Panzerkampfwagen (PzKpfw) – armored fighting vehicle – 38(t) began life as the Czech-designed LT vz 38, although none had entered service with the Czech Army prior to the German occupation of Czechoslovakia in 1938. More than 1400 were built for the Axis forces between 1939 and 1942. When it became outclassed as a light tank, the type was used as a reconnaissance vehicle and the chassis was used as the basis for a large number of vehicles, including the Marder tank destroyer, several self-propelled anti-aircraft guns, a weapons carrier and the Hetzer tank destroyer, which stayed in service with the Swiss Army until the late 1960s. During its combat career its armor thickness steadily increased. For example, the Ausf E version onwards had armor 2 in (50 mm) thick.

Conventional tank design

Basically, the PzKpfw 38(t) (LT-38) was a conventional pre-WWII tank design, with riveted armor and rear-mounted engine. The centrally located two-man turret housed the main armament, a Skoda A7 gun and a 0.32 in (7.92 mm) machine gun. A second machine gun of similar caliber, manned by the radio operator, was mounted in the forward hull next to the driver.

Production of the LT-38 continued after the German occupation, the tank being designated PzKpfw 38(t) for use by the Wehrmacht as well as Germany's satellites, Hungary, Slovakia, Romania and Bulgaria.

Infantry Tank Matilda

Before production ceased in August 1943, 2987 Matildas were produced, the Mk II suffix being dropped as the earlier Mk I disappeared from first-line service. It was the best British tank in service in 1940.

The Matilda II was not a fast tank and was seriously under-gunned, even by the standards of 1940, but it was mechanically reliable.

COUNTRY OF ORIGIN: United Kingdom	
CREW: 4	
WEIGHT: 59,237 lb (26,926 kg)	
DIMENSIONS: length 18 ft 5 in (5.613 m); width 8 ft 6 in (2.59 m); height 8 ft 3 in (2.51 m)	
RANGE: 160 miles (257 km)	
ARMOR: 0.8–3.1 in (20–78 mm)	
ARMAMENT: one 2-pounder gun; one 0.31 in (7.92 mm) Besa machine gun	
POWERPLANT: two Leyland 6-cylinder petrol engines each developing 95 hp (71 kW) or two AEC diesels each developing 87 hp (65 kW)	
PERFORMANCE: maximum speed 15 mph (24 km/h); maximum cross-country speed 8 mph (12.9 km/h); fording 3 ft 0 in (0.914 m); vertical obstacle 2 ft (0.609 m); trench 7 ft (2.133 m)	

The Mk I Matilda was developed in response to a 1934 requirement for an infantry tank. Well armored for its day, it was a small, simple tank. Because of the thickness of its armor, the Matilda proved virtually immune to the fire of the German tanks it encountered in France, and in one memorable action at Arras on May 21, 1940, 16 Matilda IIs, backed up by 58 of the smaller machine-gun-armed Mk Is, severely disrupted the advance of General Erwin Rommel's 7th Panzer Division. The British attack was only halted when the Matildas came up against 3.46 in (88 mm) anti-aircraft guns, hastily turned into anti-tank weapons on

Rommel's orders. The Mk II had improved armament and this helped the Matilda to fare reasonably well in combat, particularly in North Africa where it was widely used in the run-up to El Alamein in 1942.

Undertaking specialized tank roles

Following its replacement in front-line service, the Matilda was used for a variety of specialized roles, such as mine-clearing (the Baron); as a flame-thrower tank (the Frog); and as the basis of a Canal Defense Light for illuminating night operations.

The Matilda II was the only British tank with enough armor to withstand German anti-tank projectiles in the early years of World War II. It fought in France and the Western Desert.

KV-1 Heavy Tank

The Klim-Voroshilov KV-1 was the most formidable tank in the world when it first appeared in 1941. It took its name from Klimenti Voroshilov, then the Soviet Commissar for Defense.

COUNTRY OF ORIGIN: USSR

CREW: 5

WEIGHT: 94,600 lb (43,000 kg)

DIMENSIONS: length 21 ft 11 in (6.68 m); width 10 ft 10.7 in (3.32 m); height 8 ft 10.7 in (2.71 m)

RANGE: 93.2 miles (150 km)

ARMOR: 3.94 in (100 mm)

ARMAMENT: one 3 in (76.2 mm) gun; four 0.30 in (7.62 mm) machine guns

POWERPLANT: one V–2K V–12 diesel engine developing 600 hp (448 kW)

PERFORMANCE: maximum (rarely achieved) road speed 21.75 mph (35 km/h); fording not known; vertical obstacle 3 ft 8 in (1.20 m); trench 8 ft 6 in (2.59 m)

A KV-1 on its way to the front through the streets of Moscow, December 1941.

Design on the KV-1 began in 1938, as a successor to the T-35 heavy tank. It was evaluated under operational conditions in the war with Finland, and ordered into production as the KV-1A, with a long-barrel 3 in (76.2 mm) gun, and KV-2 with a 4.8 in (122 mm) main armament, which made the tank too ponderous to be much use. It also had a tall, slab-sided turret which was a tempting target for enemy gunners, and rendered the tank vulnerable. Nevertheless, the KV-1 set the standard for Soviet tank design for several years to come and proved to be a formidable vehicle, being used as an assault tank or to spearhead breakthroughs.

Automotive problems

However, the tank was not particularly mobile and suffered from automotive problems. In addition, it was uparmored progressively without any increase in power, which resulted in poor power-to-weight ratio and performance. The importance of the KV-1 is that it paved the way for later generations of Russian heavy tanks, such as the Josef Stalin.

The Soviet KV-1 heavy tank was the most powerful tank in the world when it first appeared.

Hotchkiss H-39

The last in a series of light armored fighting vehicles developed by Hotchkiss in the 1930s, the H-39 was fast and agile, but could not withstand the guns of the Panzers.

COUNTRY OF ORIGIN: France

CREW: 2

WEIGHT: 26,620 lb (12,100 kg)

DIMENSIONS: length 13 ft 10 in (4.22 m); width 6 ft 4.8 in (1.95 m); height 7 ft 0.6 in (2.15 m)

RANGE: 74.5 miles (120 km)

ARMOR: 1.57 in (40 mm)

ARMAMENT: one 1.46 in (37 mm) gun; one coaxial 0.30 in (7.5 mm) machine gun

POWERPLANT: one Hotchkiss six-cylinder petrol engine developing 120 hp (89.5 kW)

PERFORMANCE: maximum road speed 22.3 mph (36 km/h); fording 2 ft 10 in (0.85 m); vertical obstacle 1 ft 8 in (0.50 m); trench 5 ft 11 in (1.80 m)

The Hotchkiss light tanks equipped many French cavalry units during the Battle of France. They were no match for the German armor.

The Hotchkiss H-39 first appeared in 1939, intended for use by French cavalry formations. Despite production problems common to all French tanks in the period before World War II, around 1000 were built. About 100 of the H-39 variant had been delivered to the French armored units at the time of the German invasion; total production of the H-38 and H-39 was 890 units, together with 400 of the earlier H-35. The two later variants could be distinguished from the H-35 by their raised rear decking, which was flat instead of being sloped. The tank did well in combat during the German invasion of France in 1940, but had too little firepower to compete with enemy armor. Also, French tactics envisaged tanks being used as infantry support rather than in mass formations, diminishing its effectiveness.

Occupation duties

After the surrender, the Germans used the H-39 for occupation duties. Some saw action with the Free French and Vichy French forces in the Middle East, where they were later used by the Israelis, remaining in service until 1956.

Armed with the SA38 1.46 in (37 mm) L33 gun, the Hotchkiss H-39 had a respectable performance by 1930s standards. Its biggest disadvantage was that its commander also had to operate the gun.

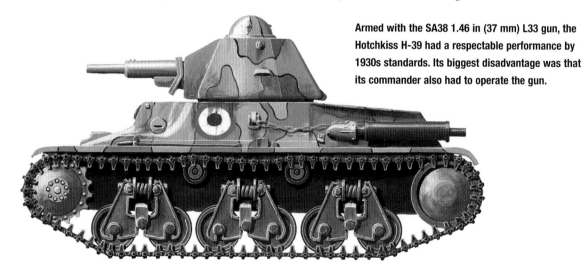

Fiat L6/40

The L6/40 was a product of the Italian Army's preference for light cavalry tanks at the expense of medium tanks, which would have been a much better proposition.

COUNTRY OF ORIGIN: Italy

CREW: 2

WEIGHT: 14,960 lb (6800 kg)

DIMENSIONS: length 12 ft 5 in (3.78 m); width 6 ft 4 in (1.92 m); height 6 ft 8 in (2.03 m)

RANGE: 124 miles (200 km)

ARMOR: 0.23–1.57 in (6–40 mm)

ARMAMENT: one Breda Model 35 0.79 in (20 mm) cannon; one coaxial Breda Model 38 0.31 in (8 mm) machine–gun

POWERPLANT: one SPA 18D four-cylinder petrol engine developing 70 hp (52 kW)

PERFORMANCE: maximum road speed 26 mph (42 km/h); fording 2 ft 8 in (0.8 m); vertical obstacle 2 ft 4 in (0.7 m); trench 5 ft 7 in (1.7 m)

The Fiat L6/40 arose from a 1930s design based on the British Carden-Loyd Mark VI tankette. Intended primarily for export, the first production models arrived in 1939 and a total of 283 were built. The tank had a lengthy gestation period, several prototypes (all with different armament configurations) being produced in the late 1930s. The first had a sponson-mounted 1.46 in (37 mm) gun, and another had twin 0.31 in (8 mm) machine guns. Finally, the turret-mounted Breda Modello 35 was selected, and

Australian troops inspect a knocked-out L6/40 light tank in the desert. The L6/40 also saw action in the USSR.

the tank was built as the Carro Armato L6/40. At its introduction, the L6/40 was nearly equal to the German PzKpfw II, but was never really suitable for front-line service. However, it saw service with reconnaissance and cavalry units in Italy, North Africa and Russia.

No chance against Allied armor

Variants included a flame-thrower version and a command tank, the latter having extra communications equipment and an open-topped turret. A number of L6/40s were also converted into Semovente L40 self-propelled anti-tank guns. But, like most Italian tanks at that time, it was totally outclassed when it came up against Allied armor.

Like many other light tanks of the period, the L6/40 had an operational disadvantage in that its commander also had to act as gunner and loader.

Fiat M13/40

Although it was outclassed by modern British tanks, the Fiat M13/40 saw widespread service, many abandoned examples being captured by the Allies and used against their former owners.

COUNTRY OF ORIGIN: Italy	
CREW: 4	
WEIGHT: 30,800 lb (14,000 kg)	
DIMENSIONS: length 16 ft 2 in (4.92 m); width 7 ft 3 in (2.2 m); height 7 ft 10 in (2.38 m)	
RANGE: 125 miles (200 km)	
ARMOR: 0.24–1.65 in (6–42 mm)	
ARMAMENT: one 1.85 in (47 mm) gun; two Modello 38 0.31 in (8 mm) machine guns (one coaxial, one anti-aircraft)	
POWERPLANT: one SPA TM40 eight-cylinder diesel engine developing 125 hp (93 kW)	
PERFORMANCE: maximum road speed 20 mph (32 km/h); fording 3 ft 3 in (1.0 m); vertical obstacle 2 ft 8 in (0.8 m); trench 6 ft 11 in (2.1 m)	

The Fiat 13/40 fell into British hands in some numbers after the offensive of 1940–41, and was pressed into service.

The M13/40 was based on an earlier design, the M11/39, which was not built in numbers as it was considered obsolete by the time of its introduction. The M13/40 used the same chassis but had a redesigned hull with better armor. Nearly 800 were produced in total and the tank was widely used in North Africa during Italian attempts to drive British and Commonwealth forces out of the region. In combat the M13/40 proved to be cramped and unreliable, and it caught fire easily when hit by anti-tank rounds. Many abandoned and captured M13/40s were pressed into service by the British and Australian forces and used to fill a serious shortage of Allied tanks in early 1941. The Australian 6th Cavalry Regiment had three squadrons of captured M13/40ss, which they named Dingo, Wombat and Rabbit.

Shortfall solution

For identification purposes, to try to eliminate the danger of being hit by friendly fire, the captured tanks had large white kangaroos painted on their hulls and turrets. They did not remain in Allied service for long.

The M13/40 was widely used in both the Western Desert and the Balkans, taking part in the Greek campaign and in operations against Yugoslav partisans.

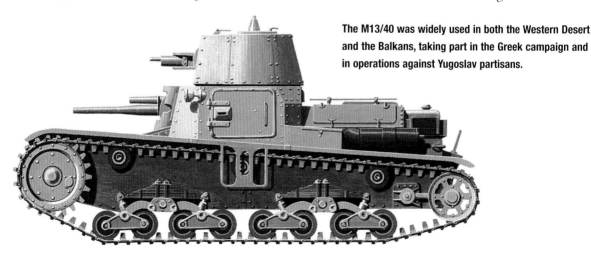

Infantry Tank Mk III Valentine

The Mk III Valentine saw action in every theater of war, and was one of the more successful pre-war tank designs. It was first used in the Western Desert in 1941.

COUNTRY OF ORIGIN: United Kingdom

CREW: 3

WEIGHT: 38,918 lb (17,690 kg)

DIMENSIONS: length 17 ft 9 in (5.41 m); width 8 ft 7.5 in (2.629 m); height 7 ft 5.5 in (2.273 m)

RANGE: 90 miles (145 km)

ARMOR: 0.3–2.6 in (8–65 mm)

ARMAMENT: one 2-pounder gun; one 3 in (7.62 mm) machine gun

POWERPLANT: one AEC diesel developing 131 hp (98 kW) in Mk III or GMC diesel developing 138 hp (103 kW) in Mk IV

PERFORMANCE: maximum speed 15 mph (24 km/h); fording 3 ft (0.914 m); vertical obstacle 2 ft 9 in (0.838 m); trench 7 ft 6 in (2.286 m)

Valentines in action in the Western Desert. One has fallen victim to the fire of a German 3.46 in (88 mm) anti-tank gun.

In 1938 Vickers was asked to produce an infantry tank based on their A10 Cruiser tank. There were doubts about the new Valentine's two-man turret, which would limit the possibility of increased armament later, but as war was imminent necessity overcame caution. Mass production began in 1940 and the Valentine soon proved to be a sturdy, reliable vehicle, if a little slow. Armament was gradually improved as the war progressed, and the Valentine saw service in all theaters. Variants included a mobile bridge, a flame-thrower tank, a mine-clearing tank and a self-propelled gun. Over 8000 Valentines were built before production ceased in 1944, making the Valentine one of the most important British tanks in numbers.

Supplying the Soviet Union

The Valentine first saw action during Operation Crusader (the British offensive to relieve Tobruk) in November 1941. The tank was also produced in Canada, most of the Canadian output being sent to the Soviet Union. Many Valentines saw service in the Burma campaign, where they were superior to the Japanese types in service.

A Valentine seen in the camouflage of the Western Desert campaign, where the tank first saw action.

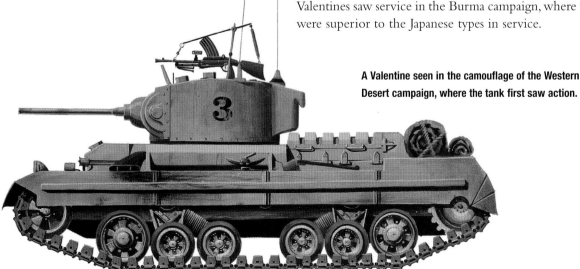

T-34 Medium Tank

When the first examples appeared in combat in the summer of 1941, the T-34 came as a profound shock to the Germans, whose armor had hitherto swept all before it.

COUNTRY OF ORIGIN: USSR

CREW: 4

WEIGHT: 57,200 lb (26,000 kg)

DIMENSIONS: length 19 ft 5.1 in (5.92 m); width 9 ft 10 in (3.0 m); height 8 ft (2.44 m)

RANGE: 115 miles (186 km)

ARMOR: 0.71–2.36 in (18–60 mm)

ARMAMENT: one 3 in (76.2 mm) gun; two 0.30 in (7.62 mm) machine guns

POWERPLANT: one V-2-34 V-12 diesel engine developing 500 hp (373 kW)

PERFORMANCE: maximum road speed 34 mph (55 km/h); fording 4 ft 6 in (1.37 m); vertical obstacle 2 ft 4 in (0.71 m); trench 9 ft 8 in (2.95 m)

The commander of a T-34 takes the salute at a military parade. The T-34 made an enormous contribution to Allied victory.

The T-34 was an advanced tank for its era, produced in vast numbers to an excellent design born of two decades of Soviet experimentation and a readiness to embrace the best of foreign ideas. Mass production began in 1940 and its powerful gun and thick armor came as a nasty surprise to the Germans in 1941–42. Finesse was sacrificed for speed of production, but their rough-and-ready appearance belied their effectiveness. The T-34 was used in every role from recovery vehicle to personnel carrier and reconnaissance, and distinguished itself at every turn, forcing the Germans back on the defensive. It is no exaggeration to say that the T-34 was the most decisive tank of World War II. An improved model, the T-34/85, appeared in 1943, and it was this version that opened the gates to the flood of Soviet armor that began to roll westward to the frontiers of Germany after the battle of Kursk in July 1943.

Replacing all others

By 1945, the T-34 had replaced nearly every other type of Russian tank in production. After World War II, T-34s equipped the armies of many countries within the Soviet sphere of influence.

The T-34/76, seen here, was instrumental in turning the tide of war on the Eastern Front. It remained in use with Soviet satellite countries long after the war.

Cruiser Tank Mk VI Crusader

Developed from the A13 Covenanter, the Mark VI Crusader played an important part in the desert war, despite being outclassed by its German counterparts. Its main weakness was its lack of adequate firepower.

The Crusader had a well-designed turret, with sloping armor, but the tank was generally outclassed by its German opponents.

COUNTRY OF ORIGIN: United Kingdom

CREW: 3

WEIGHT: 44,147 lb (20,067 kg)

DIMENSIONS: length 19 ft 8 in (5.994 m); width 8 ft 8 in (2.64 m); height 7 ft 4 in (2.235 m)

RANGE: 127 miles (204 km)

ARMOR: 1.57 in (40 mm)

ARMAMENT: one 2-pounder gun; one coaxial 0.30 in (7.62 mm) machine gun

POWERPLANT: one Nuffield Liberty Mk III petrol engine developing 340 hp (254 kW)

PERFORMANCE: maximum road speed 27 mph (43.4 km/h); maximum cross–country speed 15 mph (24 km/h); fording 3 ft 3 in (0.99 m); vertical obstacle 2 ft 3 in (0.686 m); trench 8 ft 6 in (2.59 m)

The Mk VI Crusader tank was designed and built by Nuffield, who took the A13 Covenanter as the basis of an improved design, the A15. The A15 prototype had two small auxiliary forward turrets, each with a machine gun, but these were eliminated in the production version. The new tank also had five road wheels on either side (Covenanter had four). However, by the time the Crusader first appeared in 1941 it was already outdated.

Fast but unreliable

Fast and mobile (their suspension was so tough theoretical maximum speed was often exceeded), they were thinly armored and lacked firepower, being no match for their German counterparts. Reliability was also a problem. Even with gradual improvements, the Crusader failed to prove itself in the North African campaigns and was replaced as quickly as possible by the M4 Sherman. Once withdrawn from front-line combat duties, the Crusader was adapted for a variety of roles, such as anti–aircraft tank, recovery vehicle and combat enginner tank with a dozer blade. Many saw service in the last years of the war as artillery tractors, pulling the 17-pounder gun.

The Crusader was eventually armed with a more effective gun, the 6-pounder. Its other main asset was its suspension, which was so tough that the tank could often exceed its designed maximum speed.

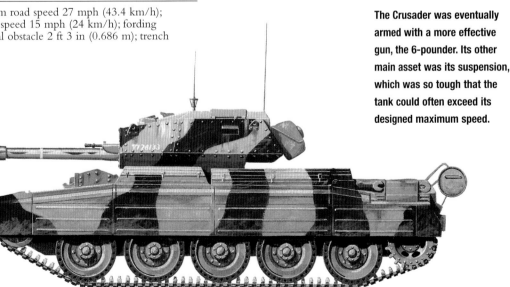

Mk VII Tetrarch (A17)

Initially rejected by the British Army as a light tank, the A17 Mk VII Tetrarch found a new lease of life as a reconnaissance tank for the newly formed airborne forces in 1941.

The small size of the air-portable Tetrarch is indicated by the soldier standing next to it.

COUNTRY OF ORIGIN: United Kingdom	
CREW: 3	
WEIGHT: 7.5 tons (7620 kg)	
DIMENSIONS: length 13 ft 6 in (4.11 m); width 7 ft 7 in (2.31 m); height 6 ft 11 in (2.10 m)	
RANGE: 140 miles (225 km)	
ARMOR: 0.16–0.55 in (4–14 mm)	
ARMAMENT: one 2pdr (1.57 in/40 mm) gun; one 0.31 in (7.92 mm) Besa MG	
POWERPLANT: Meadows Flat-12 petrol developing 165 hp (123 kW) at 2700 rpm	
PERFORMANCE: maximum speed 39.74 mph (64 km/h); fording: 3 ft (0.91 m); trench: 5 ft (1.52 m)	

The A17 Tetrarch, initially called the Purdah, started life as a private venture of the Vickers Company. The prototype underwent trials in 1938, and despite making a fairly poor showing, and lacking adequate armor and armament, it was ordered into production in 1940 as a reconnaissance vehicle. However, following an appraisal of the poor performance of light tanks in action, production was stopped until 1941, when the A17 was adopted by the newly established airborne forces.

Hamilcar and Tetrarch

At the same time, Specification (X.27/40) was issued for a large glider to airlift the tank. This resulted in the General Aircraft Hamilcar, which first flew in March 1942, and was given the name Tetrarch in 1943. The combination of Hamilcar and Tetrarch went into action on the night of June 5/6, 1944, when

the gliders landed on the River Orne with elements of the Airborne Armored Reconnaissance Regiment. The Tetrarch was also used in Operation Varsity, the crossing of the Rhine at Wesel in March 1944, where the task of the British 6th Airborne Division was to secure the northern part of the assault area, to seize the high ground east of Bergen and bridges over the River Issel, to capture the town of Hamminkeln and protect the northern flank of the US XVIII Airborne Corps. The use of the Tetrarchs undoubtedly helped the 6th Airborne Division to seize its objectives with great speed, despite suffering heavy losses.

The Tetrarch was first deployed by British airborne forces during the Normandy landings.

M.41

The Semovente M.41 was a powerful anti-tank weapon, and was much respected by the Allies in the North African campaign. Only the driver was protected by all-round armor.

COUNTRY OF ORIGIN: Italy	
CREW: 2 (on gun)	
WEIGHT: 37,400 lb (17,000 kg)	
DIMENSIONS: length 17 ft 0.9 in (5.205 m); width 7 ft 2.6 in (2.20 m); height 7 ft 0.6 in (2.15 m)	
RANGE: 124 miles (200 km)	
ARMOR: none	
ARMAMENT: one 3.54 in (90 mm) cannon	
POWERPLANT: one SPA 15-TM-41 eight-cylinder petrol engine developing 145 hp (108.1 kW)	
PERFORMANCE: maximum road speed 22 mph (35.5 km/h); fording 3 ft 3 in (1.0 m); vertical obstacle 35.4 in (0.9 m); trench 6 ft 10.7 in (2.1 m)	

The M.41 was not much use in its intended role in hilly country, but was effective as a long-range artillery weapon.

The M.41 was the only heavy tank destroyer produced by Italy during World War II. Using the chassis of the M 14/41 tank, designers mounted a powerful anti-aircraft gun on the vehicle. To accommodate the gun mounting the engine was moved to the front of the chassis and the gun was rear-mounted. In action, two men sat on the mounting behind a gun shield. The M.41 was essentially used as a "stand-off" weapon, picking off tank targets at long range. No ammunition was carried on the vehicle itself, which had to be supported by a specially converted L6 light tank ammunition carrier, with 26 rounds. Designed to operate at long range, the M.41 was not thought to need armor protection. The first production vehicles appeared in 1941, but only 48 were ever built, mainly because Italy's industrial plant was limited, but also because the gun was required for regular anti-aircraft duties.

Long-range artillery

The M.41 proved effective in the open spaces of North Africa, but after being seized by the Germans after the Italian surrender proved to have little value in the mountainous terrain of Italy, where few tanks could operate. Most were therefore used as long-range artillery.

The most powerful version of the M.41 tank destroyer was the M.41M. It was every bit as effective as the German 3.46 in (88 mm) gun and went into action in Tunisia in 1943.

M2 Light Tank

Like many other designs, the American M2 light tank was inspired by the Vickers 6-ton (6096 kg) light tank of the early 1930s, and went on to see a good deal of service in the Pacific war.

COUNTRY OF ORIGIN: United States
CREW: 4
WEIGHT: 23,000 lb (11,000 kg)
DIMENSIONS: length 14 ft 7 in (4.45 m); width 8 ft 4 in (2.53 m); height 8 ft 3 in (2.52 m)
RANGE: 130 miles (209 km)
ARMOR: 0.98 in (25 mm)
ARMAMENT: one 1.46 in (37 mm) Gun M5; five 0.30 in (7.62 mm) Browning M19194 machine guns
POWERPLANT: Continental W-670-9A, 7-cylinder, 245/220 hp (183/164 kW)
PERFORMANCE: maximum road speed 34 mph (55 km/h)

Early US light tank designs culminated in the M2, which formed the basis of a whole family of American tanks.

The M2 light tank was developed by the Rock Island Arsenal in the mid-1930s, using the Vickers 6-ton (6096 kg) light tank as a design platform. It was intended for use as an infantry support vehicle, particularly by the US Marine Corps. The first ten units were delivered with single turrets, but subsequent vehicles were delivered with a twin-turret configuration, with a 0.30 in (7.62 mm) machine gun in the second turret a layout that was favored by light tank designers of the 1930s, especially those influenced by the Vickers designs. The vehicle was progressively upgraded during its early years in service, but after the outbreak of war in Spain, closely followed by conflict in China and Europe, where US observers saw how British and French light tanks were decimated by the German panzers, the US military realized that it was no longer adequate and ordered development of the M3, based on the M2 series but with heavier armor and a slightly longer hull.

Supporting the US Marine Corps

Production switched from the M2A4 to the M3 in 1941 and the type saw much service in the early campaigns in the Pacific, particularly in support of the US Marine Corps fighting for possession of Guadalcanal. Some M3s were also purchased by Britain, together with about 30 M2A4s.

The M2 saw widespread service in the early months of the Pacific war, where it was used in support of US amphibious forces in their "island-hopping" campaigns.

T-37

Although the Russian T-37 drew its inspiration from the Carden-Loyd Tankette, it was not a copy. The Russians took the best features of the British vehicle and improved on them.

COUNTRY OF ORIGIN: USSR

CREW: 2

WEIGHT: 3.15 tons (3200 kg)

DIMENSIONS: length 12 ft 3 in (3.75 m); width 6 ft 11 in (2.1 m); height 5 ft 6 in (1.82 m)

RANGE: 115 miles (185 km)

ARMOR: 0.157 in (4 mm) hull, 0.354 in (9 mm) turret

ARMAMENT: one 0.3 in (7.62 mm) DT MG

POWERPLANT: GAZ AA 4-cylinder petrol, 65 hp (48.5 kW) at 2200 rpm

PERFORMANCE: maximum speed 35 mph (56.3 km/h)

The T-37 light amphibious tank was produced in several different versions from 1935 onwards and suffered huge losses in 1941.

The inspiration for the T-37 light amphibious reconnaissance vehicle was Britain's Carden-Loyd AE 11 amphibious tankette, several of which were purchased by the USSR in 1931. The T-37 was not a copy of the British AFV, which the Russians used as the basis for a much developed version. This resulted in the T-33, which was put to trial and found to be unsatisfactory. After substantial redesign, the vehicle emerged as the T-37. It entered production in 1933 with several major improvements incorporated into it, such as a suspension based on that of the French AMR 33 light tank. Production continued until 1936, the T-37 being built in several versions.

Taking on superior armor

One of the most important of these was the T-37TU command vehicle, which was equipped with a large radio frame aerial around the upper hull; in due course this was replaced by a pole aerial. Despite the fact that it was obsolescent, the T-37 was used in combat during the early stages of Operation Barbarossa in 1941, sometimes engaging vastly superior German armor. It had largely gone from front-line service by the spring of 1942, together with the model T-38. Some T-37s served with the Romanian Army until at least November 1942.

Although not very effective as an infantry support tank, the T-37 performed an important role as a command vehicle, the T-37TU.

Marder II

The Marder II was a conversion of the obsolete Panzer II and was developed to counter the Soviet T-34 medium tank.

COUNTRY OF ORIGIN: Germany

CREW: 3 or 4

WEIGHT: 24,200 lb (11,000 kg)

DIMENSIONS: length 20 ft 10.4 in (6.36 m); width 7 ft 5.8 in (2.28 m); height 7 ft 2.6 in (2.20 m)

RANGE: 118 miles (190 km)

ARMOR: 0.39 in (10 mm)

ARMAMENT: one 2.95 in (75 mm) Pak 40/2 gun; one 0.31 in (7.92 mm) MG34 machine gun

POWERPLANT: one Maybach HL 62 petrol engine developing 140hp (104.4kW)

PERFORMANCE: maximum road speed 24.8 mph (40 km/h); fording 2 ft 11 in (0.9 m); vertical obstacle 1 ft 4 in (0.42 m); trench 5 ft 11 in (1.8 m)

The Marder II was one of the more important Panzerjäger conversions, and was produced for service on all fronts.

In the later summer of 1941, with the appearance of the Soviet T-34 medium tank on the Eastern Front, the Wehrmacht's requirement for a powerful, mobile and dedicated tank destroyer assumed a new urgency. As an interim measure, it was decided to mount anti-tank guns on the bases of such vehicles like the obsolete Panzer II and captured vehicles like the Tracteur Blindé 37L Lorraine. The result was the Marder series, whose vehicles were armed either with the 2.95 in (75 mm) PaK (Panzer Abwehr Kanone) 40 or the captured Russian 0.30 in (7.62 mm) F22 field gun. The Marder I, developed in May 1942, carried the PaK 1.57 in (40 mm) gun, mounted in an open-topped crew compartment on a Lorraine chassis. About 170 Marder Is were built, some being conversions of French Hotchkiss and FCM light tanks. The Panzer II conversion was known as the Marder II.

Firepower and mobility

The combination of firepower and mobility worked well and the Marder II as it was known remained in production until 1944, with 1217 being made. The Marder II saw action in all theaters, particularly on the Eastern Front, where some were later equipped with infrared systems for night-fighting. The Marder II proved an effective and versatile weapon and was the most widely used German self-propelled gun of World War II. A further conversion, the Marder III, which was deployed on all fronts, was based on the Panzerkampfwagen PzKpfw 38(t).

The Marder II was numerically one of the most important German tank-destroyers, but its profile was rather high and it lacked protection. It was deployed mostly on the Eastern Front.

T-40

The T-40 was designed to replace the T-37, whose manifold deficiencies had become painfully apparent by 1938.

By the late 1930s the Red Army had invested heavily in the light tank concept. One such model was the T-40.

COUNTRY OF ORIGIN: USSR	
CREW: 2	
WEIGHT: 12,980 lb (5900 kg)	
DIMENSIONS: length 13 ft 5.8 in (4.11 m); width 7 ft 7.7 in (2.33 m); height 6 ft 4.8 in (19.5 m)	
RANGE: 224 miles (360 km)	
ARMOR: 0.3–0.55 in (8–14 mm)	
ARMAMENT: one 0.50 in (12.7 mm) machine gun	
POWERPLANT: one GAZ-202 petrol engine developing 70 hp (52.2 kW)	
PERFORMANCE: maximum speed 27.3 mph (44 km/h); fording: amphibious; vertical obstacle 2 ft 3.6 in (0.70 m); trench 10 ft 2.8 in (3.12 m)	

The T-40 was designed at the Moscow Factory No. 37, where two earlier AFV, the T-30A and T-30B, had been built. The first was amphibious and was built as the T-40; the second, designated T-40S, was a dry-land version. In the event it proved too heavy and was abandoned. The T-30B prototype, married to a T-40 chassis, became the T-60. To speed development, the design included as many automobile components as possible. Flotation tanks were installed at the rear, giving the tank a bulky appearance. The T-40 was equipped with very thin armor and fared

poorly as a result during the fighting in Finland in 1939. It was thus decided to dispense with the amphibious characteristics and use the vehicle as a land tank.

Of minimal use only

This proved an impractical conversion and its use was minimal after that, seeing some service with armored formations as a reconnaissance vehicle during 1941 against the Germans. Only around 225 T-40s were ever built, as light tanks were given low priority at that time.

By the time of the German invasion in 1941, the era of the Russian light tank was over, and heavy armor was the order of the day.

M3 Stuart (Light Tank M3)

The M3A1 light tank was the main combat version of the M2/M3 light tank series in service with the US Army at the time of the Japanese attack on Pearl Harbor in December 1941. It took part in the Pacific Islands campaigns.

The M3A1 was much modified during the course of its active career. It was immensely popular with its crews.

COUNTRY OF ORIGIN: United States	
CREW: 4	
WEIGHT: 28,440 lb (12,927 kg)	
DIMENSIONS: length 14 ft 10.75 in (4.54 m); width 7 ft 4 in (2.24 m); height 7 ft 6.5 in (2.30 m)	
RANGE: 70 miles (112.6 km)	
ARMOR: 0.59–1.69 in (15–43 mm)	
ARMAMENT: one 1.46 in (37 mm) gun; two 0.30 in (7.7 mm) machine guns	
POWERPLANT: one Continental W-970-9A six-cylinder radial petrol engine developing 250 hp (186.5 kW)	
PERFORMANCE: maximum road speed 36 mph (58 km/h); fording 3 ft 0 in (0.91 m); vertical obstacle 2 ft (0.61 m); trench 6 ft (1.83 m)	

Having followed the battles of 1940 on the European mainland closely, the American military realized that its main light tank, the M2, was obsolete, and a more heavily armored version was required. The result was the M3. It entered full-scale production in 1941, and nearly 6000 were built. Many were passed to the Soviet Red Army and to British forces. It was the British who named it the Stuart, after the Civil War General Jeb Stuart.

High praise for handling

About 170 Stuart tanks took part in Operation Crusader, the desert battle of November 1941, and although British tank crews complained about the weakness of its 1.46 in (37 mm) gun they praised its handling and reliability, which earned it the nickname "Honey." In US service, it first saw combat in the Philippines in

1942. The M3 was gradually replaced by an improved version with two Cadillac engines, the M5, from 1942. Their reliability and mobility were impressive. They were popular with crews, and used in all theaters of the war. Obsolete as a combat tank by 1944, many were converted to command and reconnaissance vehicles with the turrets removed and extra machine guns added instead. Variants included mine-clearing, flame-throwing and anti-aircraft versions.

The light tank M3A1 was the main combat version of the M2/M3 series in service when the United States entered the war in December 1941. It mounted a 1.46 in (37 mm) main gun, and there was provision for three machine guns.

Cruiser Tank Ram Mk I

Although Canada had no armored forces in 1939, the army was expanding rapidly and decided to build its own cruiser tank to provide infantry support. The result was the RAM tank, which in the event never saw combat.

COUNTRY OF ORIGIN: Canada	
CREW: 5	
WEIGHT: 64,864 lb (29,484 kg)	
DIMENSIONS: length 19 ft (5.79 m); width 9 ft 6 in (2.895 m); height 8 ft 9 in (2.667 m)	
RANGE: 144 miles (232 km)	
ARMOR: 1–3.5 in (25–89 mm)	
ARMAMENT: one 2-pounder gun; two coaxial 0.30 in (7.62 mm) machine guns	
POWERPLANT: one Continental R–975 radial petrol engine developing 400 hp (298 kW)	
PERFORMANCE: maximum road speed 25 mph (40.2 km/h); vertical obstacle 2 ft (0.61 m); trench 7 ft 5 in (2.26 m)	

The Ram cruiser tank started life as an emergency measure, at a time when there was little chance of obtaining tanks from the UK.

At the start of World War II, Canada had no tank units. With no possibility of obtaining tanks from a desperate Britain, the Canadians were forced to build their own. The decision was taken to use the basic components of the American M3, but swap the sponson-mounted main gun for a turret mounting the readily available 1.57 in (40 mm) gun, with the option of upgunning later.

Armored personnel carriers

The prototype Cruiser Tank Ram Mk I appeared in June 1941 and production began in November. In February 1942 production switched to the improved Ram Mk II, which was armed with a 6-pounder gun, and continued until July 1943, when the decision was taken to equip British and Canadian armored units with the M4 Sherman tank. Many Rams had their turrets removed and were used as armored personnel carriers. The Ram's greatest contribution to the Allied victory was as the basis for the Sexton self-propelled gun. After the war, about 100 Rams were taken over by the Netherlands Army, which formed its first armored units with them.

The Ram Mk 1 used the chassis of the American M3, but mounted its main armament in a turret rather than in a sponson as on the original US vehicle. It was originally equipped with a 2-pounder gun, but this was soon replaced by a much more effective 6-pounder.

L.40

The Semovente L.40 was used in some numbers by the Italian and later the German armies, and was a conversion of the L.6/40 light tank fitted with the powerful Italian 1.85 in (47 mm) anti-tank gun.

COUNTRY OF ORIGIN: Italy	
CREW: 2	
WEIGHT: 14,300 lb (6500 kg)	
DIMENSIONS: length 13 ft 1.5 in (4.00 m); width 6 ft 3.6 in (1.92 m); height 5 ft 4.2 in (1.63 m)	
RANGE: 124 miles (200 km)	
ARMOR: 0.23–1.65 in (6–42 mm)	
ARMAMENT: one Böhler 1.85 in (47 mm) gun or 0.31 in (8 mm) Breda modelo 38 machine gun	
POWERPLANT: one SPA 18D four-cylinder petrol engine developing 68 hp (50.7 kW)	
PERFORMANCE: maximum road speed 26.3 mph (42.3 km/h); fording 2 ft 7 in (0.8 m); vertical obstacle 2 ft 7 in (0.8 m); trench 5 ft 7 in (1.7 m)	

The L.40, seen here as a museum piece, was reasonably successful as an anti-armor weapon, but it lacked protection.

The Italians were ahead of tactical thinking in one aspect of armored vehicle production, when they developed one of the first tank destroyers in the late 1930s. This thinking proved useful when it was realized that their light tanks were of little combat value in North Africa in 1941. The chassis of the Semovente M 40 was fitted with a Böhler 1.85 in (47 mm) gun, one of the hardest hitting anti-tank weapons of its day, and around 280 of the tank destroyer vehicles were produced. The L.40 went into action in the Western Desert in 1942, and proved effective against British light tanks, but its poorly protected crew was still vulnerable to counter-fire. Some were provided with overhead protection later and served with the Italian forces on the Russian Front.

Unsuitable for the Italian terrain

Pressed into service by the Germans after the Italian surrender in 1943, the vehicle was unsuited for much of the Italian terrain and saw little action. Many had their armament removed and were converted into mobile command posts.

In designing the Semovente L.40 the Italians attempted to mount an anti-tank gun on a light tank chassis. Although it was successful in trials, it suffered from a lack of crew protection in combat and was soon replaced.

T-70

Although the T-70 was quite a useful reconnaissance vehicle, its 1.77 in (45 mm) gun was wholly inadequate against most German tanks and its armor was too thin.

The original T-70 used a twin-engine power train that would never have worked in action. It was soon replaced.

COUNTRY OF ORIGIN: USSR	
CREW: 2	
WEIGHT: 20,608 lb (9367 kg)	
DIMENSIONS: length 14 ft 0.9 in (4.29 m); width 7 ft 7.3 in (2.32 m); height 6 ft 8.3 in (2.04 m)	
RANGE: 223.7 miles (360 km)	
ARMOR: 0.39–2.36 in (10–60 mm)	
ARMAMENT: one 1.77 in (45 mm) gun; one 0.30 in (7.62 mm) machine gun	
POWERPLANT: two GAZ-202 petrol engines delivering a total of 140 hp (104 kW)	
PERFORMANCE: maximum road speed 28 mph (45 km/h); fording not known; vertical obstacle 2 ft 3.6 in (0.70 m); trench 10 ft 2.8 in (3.12 m)	

The T-70 light tank was an attempt to combine the roles of the T-60 reconnaissance tank and the T-50 infantry support tank. It was produced between March 1942 and October 1943, and 8226 were built.

Puny armament

The first batch of T-70s had a GAZ-202 automotive engine on either side of the hull, one driving each track, but this was soon redesigned with the engines in line on the tank's right-hand side, with normal transmission and differential.

The T-70 was armed with a puny 1.77 in (45 mm) L/46 gun with 45 rounds of ammunition, the gun being loaded and fired by the tank commander. This made commanding a tank platoon virtually impossible, as the commander had to devote his time to acquiring targets and loading and firing both the main armament and the machine gun, as well as issuing orders to his driver. A development, the T-80, which featured a two-man turret, was produced in small numbers, its run being terminated when all light tank production was cancelled in October 1943.

The T-70 was disappointing in action, and this reinforced the opinion of Soviet armored commanders that the light tank was obsolete. The production of light tanks ended in 1943.

M10

The M10 was produced in greater numbers than any other fighting vehicle of its kind, and formed the main armament of the US Army's tank destroyer battalions. It was also used by the British, French and Italians.

COUNTRY OF ORIGIN: United States

CREW: 5

WEIGHT: 65,861 lb (29,937 kg)

DIMENSIONS: length 22 ft 5 in (6.83 m); width 10 ft (3.05 m); height 8 ft 5 in (2.57 m)

RANGE: 200 miles (322 km)

ARMOR: 0.47–1.46 in (12–37 mm)

ARMAMENT: one 3 in (76.2 mm) M7 gun; one 0.50 in (12.7 mm) Browning machine gun

POWERPLANT: two General Motors six-cylinder diesel engines each developing 375 hp (276.6 kW)

PERFORMANCE: maximum road speed 32 mph (51 km/h); fording 3 ft (0.91 m); vertical obstacle 18 in (0.46 m); trench 7 ft 5 in (2.26 m)

Late in World War II the M10 was supplemented by the M36 version, which mounted a 3.54 in (90 mm) gun.

Just before its entry into World War II, the US Army developed a concept to defeat fast-moving armored formations using powerfully armed tank destroyers deployed en masse. The M10 was a product of this concept.

Destroyer battalions become assault forces

Based on the M4 Sherman tank chassis and using the M7 gun, the M10 was lightly armed as it was not intended for close-quarter combat. Production ran from September to December 1942, with nearly 5000 built. Most were issued to the US Army's tank destroyer battalions, of which there were 106 at the beginning of 1943, but the M10 also served with the British Army, who named it the Wolverine, and later on the Free French and Italian Co-Belligerent forces. The British fitted the excellent 17-pounder anti-tank guns to some of their M10s, which were then named Achilles. The concept of separate tank destroyer battalions was soon proved ineffective, and thus most M10s were used more as assault forces. The M10 served until the end of the war, but its large, bulky nature and the diminishing effect of its gun reduced its usefulness.

The M10 was intended to be the principal weapon in the armory of the US Army's Tank Destroyer Command. Although relatively lightly armored, the M10 was fast and agile. In British Army service the M10 was called the Wolverine.

Medium Tank M4A2 Sherman

With the M4 Sherman, the US Army at last had a tank to match the German Panzer IVF. It was the first truly effective combat tank produced by the United States, and was greatly superior to its predecessor, the M3.

COUNTRY OF ORIGIN: United States

CREW: 5

WEIGHT: 69,000 lb (31,360 kg)

DIMENSIONS: length 19 ft 4 in (5.9 m); width 8 ft 7 in (2.6 m); height 9 ft (2.74 m)

RANGE: 100 miles (161 km)

ARMOR: 0.59–2.99 in (15–76 mm)

ARMAMENT: one 2.95 in (75 mm) gun; one coaxial 0.30 in (7.62 mm) machine gun; 0.50 in (12.7 mm) anti-aircraft gun on turret

POWERPLANT: twin General Motors 6-71 diesel engines developing 500 hp (373 kW)

PERFORMANCE: maximum road speed 29 mph (46.4 km/h); fording 3 ft (0.9 m); vertical obstacle 2 ft (0.61 m); trench 7 ft 5 in (2.26 m)

An M4 Sherman seen in a Belgian village during the German Ardennes offensive in the winter of 1944.

The M4 Sherman began life as the Medium Tank T6. Its upper hull was cast, which not only provided added protection but also sped up production, a definite asset at that time.

The M4 Sherman used the same basic hull and suspension as the M3, but mounted the main armament on the gun turret, not the hull. Easy to build and an excellent fighting platform, it proved to be a winner for the Allies. By the time production ceased in 1945, over 40,000 had been built.

"Tommy Cookers"

There were many variants, including engineer tanks, assault tanks, rocket launchers, recovery vehicles and mine-clearers. The petrol-engined variants were not popular, being prone to bursting into flames after being hit; in fact, the Germans, when they first encountered Shermans in British service in the Western Desert, nicknamed them "Tommy Cookers," after a portable stove used in the previous war, or "Ronsons" after the famous brand of lighter. The Sherman could be very difficult to evacuate, especially if the main gun turret came to rest at the wrong angle and prevented one or the other of the forward hatches from being opened. Though outgunned by German tanks and with insufficient armor to compete in the later stages of the war, the sheer numbers produced overwhelmed enemy armored forces. It served with some South American countries until very recently.

Medium Tank M4A3

Although the M4 Sherman was perhaps not the best tank in the world in all-round capability, its reliability and the very large numbers that were deployed more than compensated for any deficiency.

COUNTRY OF ORIGIN: United States

CREW: 5

WEIGHT: 71,024 lb (32,284 kg)

DIMENSIONS: length, with gun 24 ft 8 in (7.52 m), and over hull 20 ft 7 in (6.27 m); width 8 ft 9.5 in (2.68 m); height 11 ft 2.9 in (3.43 m)

RANGE: 100 miles (161 km)

ARMOR: 0.59–3.94 in (15–100 mm)

ARMAMENT: one 2.99 in (76 mm) gun; one 0.30 in (7.62 mm) coaxial machine gun

POWERPLANT: one Ford GAA V-8 petrol engine developing 400 or 500 hp (335.6 or 373 kW)

PERFORMANCE: maximum road speed 29 mph (47 km/h); fording 3 ft (0.91 m); vertical obstacle 2 ft (0.61 m); trench 7 ft 5 in (2.26 m)

A flame–throwing M4 Sherman in action. The Sherman was adapted to many specialist assault roles.

The M4A3 was one of the most developed of all the Sherman variants used during World War II. It differed from the M4A2 mainly in the design of its turret and suspension (using a more effective horizontal volute spring system) and in its armament, employing the larger and more powerful 2.99 in (76 mm) gun as well as having thicker armor. This particular model was the production type most favored by the US Army. Ford built 1690 A3s between June 1942 and September 1943, before ceasing tank production. Manufacture was then taken over by Grand Blanc from February 1944. Improved features included a vision cupola for the commander, a loader's hatch and so-called "wet stowage" for the ammunition.

The Sherman was very much one of the interim tank-destroyer designs, for although the gun was mounted behind armor at the front and sides the armor was relatively thin, and the top and rear were open, making the crew vulnerable.

Avoid the Tigers and Panthers

The Sherman had the edge over the Panzer IV, but it stood little chance in a one-to-one encounter with later German AFVs like the Tiger and Panther. The Sherman-equipped units suffered heavy losses when they came up against Tigers for the first time in Tunisia, a scenario that was repeated in the Normandy woods a year later, following the D-Day landings.

As was the case with the Churchill tank, numbers of Shermans were modified for special tasks, such as flame-throwing and clearing paths through minefields.

Infantry Tank Mk IV Churchill

The Churchill tank was first used in action during the abortive Dieppe landing in August 1942. It went on to become the most important AFV in the British Army.

COUNTRY OF ORIGIN: United Kingdom
CREW: 5
WEIGHT: 89,412 lb (40,642 kg)
DIMENSIONS: length 24 ft 5 in (7.442 m); width 8 ft (2.438 m); height 11 ft 4 in (3.454 m)
RANGE: 90 miles (144.8 km)
ARMOR: 0.6–4 in (16–102 mm)
ARMAMENT: one 6-pounder gun; one coaxial 0.30 in (7.62 mm) machine gun
POWERPLANT: one Bedford twin-six petrol engine developing 350 hp (261 kW)
PERFORMANCE: maximum speed 12.5 mph (20 km/h); maximum cross-country speed about 8 mph (12.8 km/h); fording 3 ft 4 in (1.016 m); vertical obstacle 2 ft 6 in (0.76 m); trench 10 ft (3.048 m)

Churchill tanks (left-hand column) moving up to the front in Normandy pass American M4 Sherman tanks.

The Churchill was slow and heavily armored. The final prototype, however, was a much lighter vehicle than had first been thought of, not unlike a World War I tank in appearance. Rushed into production at a time when invasion seemed imminent, it suffered early reliability problems and was not fully introduced until 1943.

Moving over rough terrain

Early combat experience during the Dieppe raid in 1942 was disappointing, but the Churchill proved mobile over rough terrain in North Africa. The tank really began to vindicate itself with the Mk III version, which, armed with a 6-pounder gun, was deployed to the Western Desert in time to take part in the decisive Battle of El Alamein in October 1942. It continued to prove its worth in growing measure, introducing a 2.95 in (75 mm) gun in the Mk VI version. The Mk VII first went into action in support of the Normandy landings in June 1944, and it was now that the special versions of the Churchill came into their own. The tank excelled in its specialized variants, such as the AVRE, the Crocodile flame-thrower tank, the bridge-layer and many more. The tank gave excellent service. The final Churchill was not retired until the 1960s.

This image well illustrates the Churchill's angular lines. It was a classic infantry tank, slow but heavily armored, and was more difficult to knock out than the American Sherman.

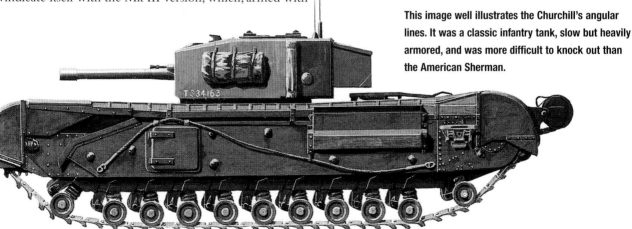

Panzer V Panther

The Panther was a technological masterpiece, and far in advance of any other tank of its day, but it had a serious drawback: it was too complex to carry out sustained operations in the field before needing servicing.

COUNTRY OF ORIGIN: Germany

CREW: 4

WEIGHT: 100,100 lb (45,500 kg)

DIMENSIONS: length 29 ft 0.75 in (8.86 m); width 11 ft 3 in (3.43 m); height 10 ft 2 in (3.10 m)

RANGE: 110 miles (177 km)

ARMOR: 1.2–4.3 in (30–110 mm)

ARMAMENT: one 2.95 in (75 mm) gun; three 0.31 in (7.92 mm) MG34 machine guns (one coaxial, one anti-aircraft, one on hull front)

POWERPLANT: one Maybach HL 230 12-cylinder diesel developing 700 hp (522 kW)

PERFORMANCE: maximum road speed 29 mph (46 km/h); fording 5 ft 7 in (1.70 m); vertical obstacle 3 ft (0.91 m); trench 6 ft 3 in (1.91 m)

A Panzer V Panther advancing in Normandy. The Panther was an excellent tank, but too complex.

The Panther is widely considered to be one of the best tanks of World War II. Designed to combat the Soviet T-34 tanks, which were outclassing the PzKpfw IV on the Eastern Front in early 1942, the Panther fulfilled the requirement for a tank with a powerful gun, good mobility and good protection. MAN completed the first production models in September 1942, but the early versions suffered from mechanical problems: at the Battle of Kursk in July 1943 only 38 out of 200 Panthers deployed with XLVIII Panzer Korps were serviceable.

Proof against frontal assault

Once the problems were ironed out, the Panther saw action in all theaters and proved effective. It was widely used in Normandy in the weeks after D-Day as well as on the Russian Front. Its sloped armor, a complete departure from earlier German tank design, was reminiscent of the T-34s. This armor, in 1943, made the Panther virtually proof against a frontal assault by any enemy high-velocity anti-tank weapon then in existence. Over 4500 were built up to early 1945, and they continued to see service with the French Army in the immediate post-war period.

Without doubt the best German tank of World War II, the Panther was hampered by its complexity, which created many problems on operations.

Panzer VI Tiger I

In 1941 the Germans produced the Tiger I tank in haste to combat the Russian KV-1, and it first saw action in the autumn of 1942. It was so impressive that it tended to dominate the enemy whenever it appeared.

The Tiger heavy tank was produced by Henschel based on a 1941 design and entered production in August 1942. A total of 1350 were built before production ceased in August 1944 and the type was replaced by the King Tiger. There were three main variants: a command tank; a recovery vehicle fitted with a winch; and the Sturmtiger, which was fitted with a rocket launcher. The Tiger was excellent but complicated and difficult to produce in large numbers and maintain. The overlapping wheel suspension had a tendency to clog with mud and stones which, if frozen, could immobilize the vehicle.

A Panzer VI Tiger I rolling across the Russian steppe prior to the Battle of Kursk in July 1943.

Four or more

It first saw action against the British in Tunisia in 1942 and then appeared on all fronts. It could knock out its most common opponents, the T-34, Sherman and Churchill IV, at ranges exceeding 1600 yards (1465 m), whereas the T-34, although it could penetrate the Tiger's side armor at a range of 500 yards (460 m) or less, could not penetrate the frontal armor at any range. The same was true of the M4 Sherman, which whenever possible engaged a Tiger in units of four tanks or more to give at least one of them a fighting chance of getting in close enough for a kill.

COUNTRY OF ORIGIN: Germany

CREW: 5

WEIGHT: 121,000 lb (55,000 kg)

DIMENSIONS: length 27 ft (8.24 m); width 12 ft 3 in (3.73 m); height 9 ft 3.25 in (2.86 m)

RANGE: 62 miles (100 km)

ARMOR: 1–3.94 in (25–100 mm)

ARMAMENT: one 3.46 in (88 mm) kwK 36 gun; one 0.31 in (7.92 mm) coaxial MG 34 machine gun

POWERPLANT: one Maybach HL 230 P45 12-cylinder petrol engine developing 700 hp (522 kW)

PERFORMANCE: maximum road speed 24 mph (38 km/h); fording 3 ft 11 in (1.20 m); vertical obstacle 2 ft 7 in (0.79 m); trench 5 ft 11 in (1.8 m)

The Tiger first saw action in Tunisia. Comparatively few, however, reached the North African theater, thanks to air and submarine attacks from Malta on the Axis supply convoys.

Cruiser Tank Mk VIII Cromwell

The Cromwell was a very effective tank in action in Normandy. Its 2.95 in (75 mm) gun gave it a good chance against German armor. The tank entered service in 1943 and many crews were trained on it before it saw combat.

COUNTRY OF ORIGIN: United Kingdom	
CREW: 5	
WEIGHT: 61,472 lb (27,942 kg)	
DIMENSIONS: length 21 ft 0.75 in (6.42 m); width 10 ft (3.048 m); height 8 ft 3 in (2.51 m)	
RANGE: 173 miles (278 km)	
ARMOR: 0.3–3 in (8–76 mm)	
ARMAMENT: one 2.95 in (75 mm) gun; one coaxial 0.30 in (7.62 mm) machine gun	
POWERPLANT: one Rolls-Royce Meteor V-12 petrol engine developing 570 hp (425 kW)	
PERFORMANCE: maximum speed 38 mph (61 km/h); fording 4 ft (1.219 m); vertical obstacle 3 ft (0.914 m); trench 7 ft 6 in (2.286 m)	

A Cromwell advancing at speed through a village in Normandy, August 1944.

The Cromwell was produced as a more heavily armed and armored tank to replace the Crusader, and the first Cromwells appeared in 1943 armed with a 6-pounder gun.

Equipped with heavier weaponry

However, the tanks were soon being equipped with heavier weaponry, which gave some parity with contemporary German tanks. That said, most units were equipped with the M4 Sherman, but the Cromwell gave valuable service as a training tank in the run-up to D-Day and was used for many other roles, such as mobile observation posts and armored recovery vehicles. Not quite equal to German tanks, the Cromwell was at least better than previous British efforts and fared well in combat. It proved to be a reliable fighting machine, especially when the 6-pounder gun that formed its original armament was replaced by the harder-hitting 2.95 in (75 mm). The version so armed was the Cromwell Mk IV, issued to the British armored regiments in October 1943. It was in the process of being replaced by the Sherman in mid-1944, yet the Cromwell saw action in Normandy with the 7th Armored Division and acquitted itself well.

The Cromwell was a neat and compact fighting vehicle, and acquitted itself well in combat.

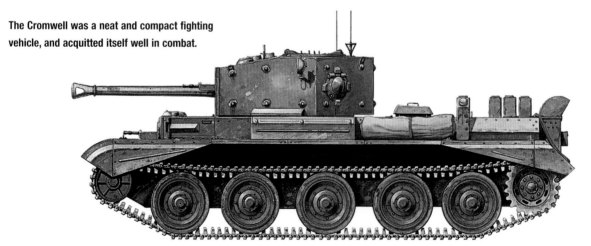

Nashorn

The Nashorn (Rhinoceros) tank destroyer was intended to be an interim measure, but proved to be one of the most successful vehicles of its kind. It was initially known as the Hornisse (Hornet).

COUNTRY OF ORIGIN: Germany	
CREW: 5	
WEIGHT: 53,680 lb (24,400 kg)	
DIMENSIONS: length 27 ft 8.3 in (8.44 m); width 9 ft 4.6 in (2.86 m); height 8 ft 8.3 in (2.65 m)	
RANGE: 130.5 miles (210 km)	
ARMOR: 0.39–1.18 in (10–30 mm)	
ARMAMENT: one 3.46 in (88 mm) Pak 43 gun; one 0.31 in (7.92 mm) MG34 machine gun	
POWERPLANT: one Maybach HL 120 petrol engine developing 265 hp (197.6 kW)	
PERFORMANCE: maximum road speed 24.8 mph (40 km/h); fording 2 ft 7.5 in (0.8m); vertical obstacle 23.6 in (0.6 m); trench 7 ft 6.6 in (2.3 m)	

Standing on a rather battered Nashorn, this British soldier gives an indication of the size of the AFV's powerful 3.46 in (88 mm) gun.

In an effort to get sizeable numbers of tank destroyers into service on the Eastern Front, the Germans embarked on a series of hurried improvisations. A special weapon-carrier vehicle based on the PzKpfw IV chassis was adapted to take the 3.46 in (88 mm) Pak 43 gun. The first of these so-called Nashorns entered service in 1943.

A long range weapon

A high vehicle, it was difficult to conceal, a problem increased by poor armor with only the driver being fully protected. It was therefore used as a long-range weapon. Some 433 were built before production ceased in 1944. The powerful gun made the Nashorn a potent battlefield weapon, but it was too bulky for its prescribed role and only the lack of anything better kept it in production in Germany. The Nashorn served on all fronts until the end of the war, and one commander, Hauptmann Albert Ernst, became an "ace" with it, destroying 14 Russian tanks in a single day in December 1943. Two Nashorns survive as museum pieces, one in the US Ordnance Museum and the other in the Kubinka Tank Museum, Moscow.

The Nashorn was very much one of the interim tank-destroyer designs, for although the gun was mounted behind armor at the front and sides the armor was relatively thin and the top and rear were open, making the crew vulnerable.

Elefant

The Germans, confronted with excellent Russian tanks, took the lead in developing effective tank destroyers. But some of their earlier designs, such as the Elefant, were cumbersome and had a disastrous combat career.

In this photograph, the Elefant's powerful 3.46 in (88 mm) gun is locked down for transit.

COUNTRY OF ORIGIN: Germany	
CREW: 6	
WEIGHT: 143,000 lb (65,000 kg)	
DIMENSIONS: length 26 ft 8 in (8.128 m); width 11 ft 1 in (3.378 m); height 9 ft 10 in (2.997 m)	
RANGE: 95 miles (153 km)	
ARMOR: 1.97–7.87 in (50–200 mm)	
ARMAMENT: one 3.46 in (88 mm) Pak 43/2 gun	
POWERPLANT: two Maybach HL 120 TRM V-12 petrol engines each developing 530 hp (395.2 kW)	
PERFORMANCE: maximum road speed 12.5 mph (20.1 km/h); fording 3 ft 4 in (1.0 m); vertical obstacle 31.5 in (0.8 m); trench 8 ft 8.3 in (2.65 m)	

The Elefant stemmed from the Porsche design for the PzKpfw VI Tiger. Henschel was awarded the contract for the new tank, but it was decided to use the Porsche design as a tank destroyer. This mounted the 3.46 in (88 mm) dual anti-tank/anti-aircraft gun in a large armored superstructure. Porsche received a contract to build 90 units under the designation Panzerjäger Tiger (P), later to become better known as either the Ferdinand or Elefant. The (P) denoted Porsche, the company of origin. Hitler demanded that the new vehicle be ready for the 1943 offensive on the Russian Front, so development was rather hurried. As a result many broke down in their first action at the Battle of Kursk, and the lack of proper armor and ponderous mobility made them easy targets for Soviet gunners.

Lack of defense

In addition, the lack of machine guns meant that there was no defense against Soviet troops disabling them with explosive charges in close-quarter combat. The survivors were withdrawn to Italy, where unreliability and lack of spares ensured their continued ineffectiveness. In practice, the slow, heavy Elefant was better suited to the role of assault gun than that of tank destroyer.

The Elefant was one of the failures of the German Panzerjäger designers. Despite its excellent main armament, it was far too cumbersome and, more importantly, the first examples lacked any kind of self-defense armament, making them vulnerable to infantry attack.

Panzer VI Tiger II

The Tiger II, sometimes called the King Tiger or Royal Tiger, was the most formidable tank to see service in World War II. Its main problem was that it lacked mobility, being slow and cumbersome.

COUNTRY OF ORIGIN: Germany

CREW: 5

WEIGHT: 153,340 lb (69,700 kg)

DIMENSIONS: length 33 ft 8 in (10.26 m); width 12 ft 3.5 in (3.75 m); height 10 ft 1.5 in (3.09 m)

RANGE: 68 miles (110 km)

ARMOR: 3.94–5.9 in (100–150 mm)

ARMAMENT: one 3.46 in (88 mm) kwK 43 gun; two 0.31 in (7.92 mm) MG34 machine guns (one coaxial, one on hull front)

POWERPLANT: one Maybach HL 230 P30 12-cylinder petrol engine developing 700 hp (522 kW)

PERFORMANCE: maximum road speed 24 mph (38 km/h); fording 5 ft 3 in (1.60 m); vertical obstacle 2 ft 10 in (0.85 m); trench 8 ft 2 in (2.5m)

The massive Tiger II was superior to any armor the Allies possessed, and only rocket-firing aircraft were a match for it.

The Henschel design for the Tiger II (King Tiger) was completed in October 1943. Early production models carried a turret designed by Porsche, but after the first 50 models had been built, the tanks were wholly produced by Henschel. The tank was similar to the Panther and used the same engine, although its heavier armor, impenetrable to most Allied weapons, resulted in a lower power-to-weight ratio and consequent loss of speed and mobility. The main problem with the Tiger II was unreliability. Many were abandoned by their crews when they broke down or ran out of fuel, as their bulk made them difficult to move or conceal. The Tiger II first saw combat on the Eastern Front in May 1944 and in the battles in Normandy in the autumn of that year.

Abandoned

With the Panther, the Tiger II formed the spearhead of the German offensive in the Ardennes in December 1944, which drove a wedge between the Allied armies. Luckily, the offensive petered out for lack of fuel and many Tigers were abandoned. In the later stages of the war, the biggest threat to the Tiger was the rocket-armed fighter-bomber.

The Tiger II was a formidable fighting machine, but it had its weak points. It could be rendered immobile by freezing mud clogging its suspension. The long-barrelled 3.46 in (88 mm) gun could fire both armor-piercing and HE ammunition.

Hetzer

A powerful vehicle for its size, the Hetzer was the best German tank destroyer to see service in World War II. It was also much cheaper to manufacture and operate than other Panzerjäger tanks.

COUNTRY OF ORIGIN: Germany

CREW: 4

WEIGHT: 31,900 lb (14,500 kg)

DIMENSIONS: length 20 ft 4.1 in (6.20 m); width 8 ft 2.4 in (2.50 m); height 6 ft 10.7 in (2.10 m)

RANGE: 155 miles (250 km)

ARMOR: 0.39–2.36 in (10–60 mm)

ARMAMENT: one 2.95 in (75 mm) Pak 39 gun; one 0.31 in (7.92 mm) MG34 machine gun

POWERPLANT: one Praga AC/2800 petrol engine developing 150–160 hp (111.9–119.3 kW)

PERFORMANCE: maximum road speed 24.2 mph (39 km/h); fording 2 ft 11 in (0.9 m); vertical obstacle 2 ft 1 in (0.65 m); trench 4 ft 3.2 in (1.3 m)

This photograph reveals the Hetzer's low silhouette. Note the "Saukopf" (pig's head) mantlet that provided extra frontal protection.

Most tank destroyer conversions of existing tank chassis were cumbersome and lacked finesse. In contrast, the various Sturmgeschütz artillery vehicles had proved very effective tank killers, so it was decided to produce a light tank destroyer along the lines of a Sturmgeschütz.

A tremendous success

Based on the PzKpfw 38(t) chassis, the new Hetzer was put into production in 1943. Small, well protected, mobile and able to knock out all but the heaviest tanks, the Hetzer

was a tremendous success. By the time the factories were overrun in May 1944, 1577 had been built, including flame-thrower and recovery versions. The combination of its very small size and low silhouette made it a difficult target to engage in battle. The Hetzer was built in Czechoslovakia after the war, some being exported to Switzerland between 1947 and 1952, where the Swiss Army continued to use them until the 1970s. The name "Hetzer" means "Baiter," signifying the AFV's role of luring tanks into a deadly trap.

The small size and low profile of the Jagdpanzer Hetzer can be readily appreciated. The "Saukopf" (pig's head) gun mantle provided extra frontal protection, and the tank lacks a muzzle brake.

Jagdpanzer IV

In the later stages of the war the Germans built some superlative tank destroyers, in particular the Jagdpanzer IV. Most Jagdpanzer IVs served on the Eastern Front, where they inflicted great losses on Soviet armor.

The Jagdpanzer IV was considered to be one of the best of its type and proved extremely effective in the battle for Berlin.

COUNTRY OF ORIGIN: Germany

CREW: 4

WEIGHT: 56,933 lb (25,800 kg)

DIMENSIONS: length 28 ft 1.8 in (8.58 m); width 9 ft 7.4 in (2.93 m); height 6 ft 5.2 in (1.96 m)

RANGE: 133 miles (214 km)

ARMOR: 0.43–3.14 in (11–80 mm)

ARMAMENT: one 2.95 in (75 mm) Pak 39 gun; two 0.31 in (7.92 mm) MG34 machine guns

POWERPLANT: one Maybach HL 120 petrol engine developing 265 hp (197.6 kW)

PERFORMANCE: maximum road speed 22 mph (35 km/h); fording 3 ft 11 in (1.2 m); vertical obstacle 23.6 in (0.6 m); trench 7 ft 6.6 in (2.3 m)

Experience during 1942 showed that the Sturmgeschütz vehicles would have to be upgunned if their role as tank destroyers was to continue. The armament of the Panther was selected, and while modifications were made to the Sturmgeschütz III to allow for this upgrade, the Panther gun was fitted to the chassis of the PzKpfw IV.

Low slung and well protected

Known as the Jagdpanzer IV, the first production models appeared in 1943. With a low silhouette and well protected hull, the Jagdpanzer IV was popular with crews,

especially as the armament could knock out almost any enemy tank. Early production Jagdpanzer IVs still had the muzzle brake. Later versions used a much longer 2.95 in (75 mm) gun, but this overloaded the chassis, and later versions also used side armor plating. The Jagdpanzer IV caused great execution among Soviet armor during the bitter fighting for the Seelow Heights in 1945, as the Red Army approached Berlin. A total of 1139 were produced between December 1943 and March 1945.

The Jagdpanzer IV was a formidable tank-killer based on the chassis of the well proven Panzer Mk IV and housed its 2.95 in (75 mm) gun in a superstructure formed from well-sloped armored plates. This is an early example with the muzzle brake and "Saukopf" (pig's head) gun mantle.

Jagdpanther

Originally named Panzerjäger Panther, this excellent tank destroyer so impressed Adolf Hitler when it was shown to him that he ordered the name changed to Jagdpanther.

COUNTRY OF ORIGIN: Germany

CREW: 5

WEIGHT: 101,200 lb (46,000 kg)

DIMENSIONS: length 32 ft 5.8 in (9.90 m); width 10 ft 8.7 in (3.27 m); height 8 ft 10.9 in (2.715 m)

RANGE: 99.4 miles (160 km)

ARMOR: 3.15–4.72 in (80–120 mm)

ARMAMENT: one 3.46 in (88 mm) Pak 43/3 gun; one 0.31 in (7.92 mm) MG34 machine gun

POWERPLANT: one Maybach HL 230 petrol engine developing 600–700 hp (447.4–522 kW)

PERFORMANCE: maximum road speed 34.2 mph (55 km/h); fording 5 ft 7 in (1.7 m); vertical obstacle 35 in (0.9 m); trench 6 ft 3 in (1.9 m)

This Jagdpanther, straight off the production line, has its tools and other stowage intact.

The Jagdpanther was one of the first purpose-built tank destroyers, as opposed to a hasty tank-conversion. Using the Panther chassis, the prototype was demonstrated to Hitler in October 1943, who named it the Jagdpanther himself. The chassis was virtually unaltered and was surmounted by a well designed armored superstructure containing a 3.46 in (88 mm) PaK 43 anti-tank gun, with an MG 34 or MG 42 machine gun for self-defense. The Jagdpanther performed exceptionally well during trials, and the enthusiasm shown for it by senior Wehrmacht officers was amply vindicated in combat. The vehicle was

superb. Fast, well armored and mounting a powerful gun, the Jagdpanther became one of the most famous of all World War II vehicles, able to knock out almost any tank it met. A machine gun and anti-magnetic mine paint helped with close-quarter defense.

A feared vehicle

On all European fronts, the Jagdpanther became feared. Fortunately for the Allies, planned production levels were never reached, and by the time the factories were overrun in April 1945, only 382 had been completed, mainly due to the disruption caused by Allied bombing raids.

The Jagdpanther was a superlative fighting vehicle and was destined to become one of the most famous armored fighting vehicles of its kind. It was not unknown for single Jagdpanthers to hold up an Allied armored advance for a considerable period of time.

Light Tank M24 Chaffee

Although it was developed during World War II, the M24 Chafee arrived too late to make a significant contribution to that conflict. It really came into its own in later battles during the early Cold War era.

COUNTRY OF ORIGIN: United States

CREW: 5

WEIGHT: 40,414 lb (18,370 kg)

DIMENSIONS: length 18 ft (5.49 m); width 9 ft 8 in (2.95 m); height 8 ft 1.5 in (2.48 m)

RANGE: 100 miles (161 km)

ARMOR: 0.47–1.5 in (12–38 mm)

ARMAMENT: one 2.95 in (75 mm) gun; two 0.30 in (7.62 mm) machine guns; one 0.50 in (12.7 mm) gun on turret; one 2.01 in (51 mm) smoke mortar

POWERPLANT: two Cadillac Model 44T24 V-8 petrol engines developing 110 hp (82 kW) each

PERFORMANCE: maximum road speed 35 mph (56 km/h); fording 3 ft 4 in (1.02 m); vertical obstacle 3 ft (0.91 m); trench 8 ft (2.44 m)

The M24 Chaffee remained in service with many countries long after the end of World War II, some being constantly updated.

By 1942 it was evident that the 1.46 in (37 mm) gun was inadequate for the needs of America's light tanks, and indeed as a main armament of any tank. Attempts to install larger weapons in M5 tanks failed and so a new tank was designed by Cadillac, the first being ready by late 1943. The gun chosen for it was a derivative of the 2.95 in (75 mm) weapon developed for the B-25H, the anti-ship version of the North American Mitchell bomber. Production of the Light Tank M24 began in 1944 and 4731 vehicles were eventually produced, some of them being allocated to the British Army. The first M24s deployed to Europe in December 1944, but did not play an important part in the last months of the war, being of small numbers and vulnerable to German tank and anti-tank guns. In Korea it realized its full combat value, with the agility for reconnaissance, but well armed.

Combat family

Its biggest contribution was in its concept. It was designed to be part of a combat family of vehicles, all using the same chassis, including self-propelled guns and anti-aircraft tanks. The tank remained in service with some nations until recently.

The M24 Chaffee light tank, armed with a 2.95 in (75 mm) gun, was introduced into service in late 1944 and formed the basis of a new family of armored fighting vehicles in the post-war years.

Archer

Some regarded the rear-facing main gun of the Archer a tactical liability, but operators of the AFV used it well by deploying the Archers in an ambush position, then making a rapid exit with the gun still trained to the rear.

COUNTRY OF ORIGIN: United Kingdom

CREW: 4

WEIGHT: 35,765 lb (16,257 kg)

DIMENSIONS: length 21 ft 11 in (6.68 m); width 9 ft 0.5 in (2.76 m); height 7 ft 4.5 in (2.25 m)

RANGE: 140 miles (225 km)

ARMOR: 0.31–2.36 in (8–60 mm)

ARMAMENT: one 17-pounder gun; one 0.303 in (7.7 mm) Bren gun

POWERPLANT: one General Motors 6-71 six-cylinder diesel engine developing 192 hp (143.2 kW)

PERFORMANCE: maximum road speed 20 mph (32.2 km/h); fording 3 ft (0.91 m); vertical obstacle 2 ft 9 in (0.84 m); trench 7 ft 9 in (2.36 m)

The Archer's rear-facing gun meant that the driver was always ready to make a fast exit from an ambush position.

The Archer stemmed from a British decision to increase anti-tank gun calibres from 2.24 in (57 mm) to 3 in (76.2 mm). The new guns were too heavy for tanks then in existence. An interim solution was found by adapting the Valentine tank chassis for use as a tank destroyer. The first production Archer, as the new vehicle was known, appeared in March 1943, but it was October 1944 before the Archer saw any action. Initial worries about the rear-facing gun proved groundless.

Ideal for ambushes

The low silhouette was ideal for ambushes, and the rear-facing gun meant that the vehicle could be driven away quickly without having to turn round, thus avoiding retaliation. The Archers were used by the anti-tank companies of the Royal Artillery, and were preferred to the weight and bulk of the towed 17-pdr guns that were also used by these companies. The end of the war brought about a halt to Archer production at a point where 655 of the original order for 800 had been produced. The Archers went on to equip British Army anti-tank units until the mid-1950s

The Archer was a conversion of the Valentine infantry tank. The first Archers were used in action in late 1944 and proved to be very useful weapons, their low silhouette being a major advantage.

M18

The M18's low silhouette, high speed and high firepower made it capable of destroying every German tank except the Tiger II, and it was an ideal vehicle for picking off enemy tanks from ambush.

COUNTRY OF ORIGIN: United States	
CREW: 5	
WEIGHT: 37,557 lb (17,036 kg)	
DIMENSIONS: length 21 ft 10 in (6.65 m); width 9 ft 5 in (2.87 m); height 8 ft 5.5 in (2.58 m)	
RANGE: 105 miles (169 km)	
ARMOR: 0.35–0.98 in (9–25 mm)	
ARMAMENT: one 3 in (76.2 mm) M1A1 gun; one 0.50 in (12.7 mm) machine gun	
POWERPLANT: one Continental R-975 C1 radial petrol engine developing 340 hp (253.5 kW)	
PERFORMANCE: maximum road speed 55 mph (88.5 km/h); fording 4 ft (1.22 m); vertical obstacle 3 ft (0.91 m); trench 6 ft 2 in (1.88 m)	

The M18 Hellcat was the only vehicle specifically designed for the US Army's tank destroyer role.

Most tank destroyers of World War II were converted tanks, but the M18 Hellcat was designed for the role. In December 1941, the US War Ordnance Department called for a fast tank destroyer using a Christie suspension, the Wright Continental R-975 engine and armed with a 1.46 in (37 mm) gun. This inadequate main armament was quickly replaced by a 2.24 in (57 mm) gun. During evaluation, it was realized that this calibre was also inadequate, so the 2.24 in (57 mm) was replaced in turn by a 2.95 in (75 mm) weapon. Development began in 1942 and the first production models appeared in 1943, over 2500 being produced before October 1944. The M18

proved to be one of the best US tank destroyers of the war. Much smaller than the M10, it carried a more powerful gun and was considerably faster, in fact being the fastest tracked vehicle of the war, a good power-to-weight ratio providing excellent agility and acceleration.

A success on the battlefield

More importantly, it was able to hold its own on the battlefield. Despite their success, the decline of enthusiasm for specialist tank destroyer units led to the M18 being used more as assault guns and artillery towards the end of the war.

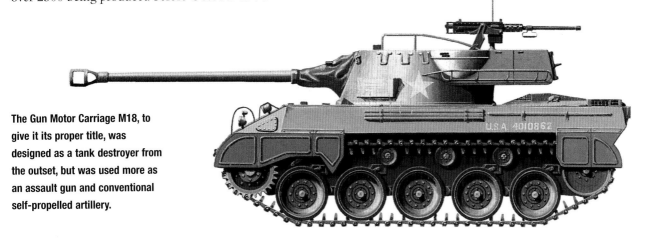

The Gun Motor Carriage M18, to give it its proper title, was designed as a tank destroyer from the outset, but was used more as an assault gun and conventional self-propelled artillery.

IS-2 Heavy Tank

The Iosif Stalin (IS) tank was named after the leader of the USSR and was developed from the KV-85, itself a version of the KV-1. The IS tanks were the most powerful in the Red Army.

COUNTRY OF ORIGIN: USSR

CREW: 4

WEIGHT: 101,200 lb (46,000 kg)

DIMENSIONS: length 32 ft 5.8 in (9.9 m); width 10 ft 1.6 in (3.09 m); height 8 ft 11.5 in (2.73 m)

RANGE: 149 miles (240 km)

ARMOR: 5.2 in (132 mm)

ARMAMENT: one 4.80 in (122 mm) gun; one 0.50 in (12.7 mm) machine gun; one 0.30 in (7.62 mm) machine gun

POWERPLANT: one V-2-IS (V-2K) V-12 diesel developing 600 hp (447 kW)

PERFORMANCE: maximum road speed 23 mph (37 km/h); fording not known; vertical obstacle 3 ft 3 in (1 m); trench 8 ft 2 in (2.49 m)

A noteworthy feature of the IS-2 was the great length of its gun. Its turret was also shaped to deflect projectiles.

The IS-2 tank, which supplanted the IS-1 in service during 1944, was the heaviest Soviet tank to be produced in World War II and the battalions equipped with it were used to batter their way through the enemy's defenses in the final assault on Berlin in April 1945.

The IS-2 (Josef Stalin) was a development of the earlier KV series of Russian tanks, and was a lighter tank with improved transmission and suspension and a redesigned hull and turret. It might also have followed the KV nomenclature, but Marshal Kliment Voroshilov had fallen out of political favor and so the new design was named Iosif (Josef) Stalin instead, the first batch, used for evaluation, being designated IS-85.

Massive, well armed and armored

The IS-1 retained the 3.34 in (85 mm) gun of the KV-85, but production models were fitted with the long 4.8 in (122 mm) gun, which had greater penetrating power and could blow off a tank's turret even if it failed to penetrate the armor. With this modification the tank became the IS-2. The first examples appeared in 1944. A massive vehicle, the tank was well armed and armored, the only drawback of the early versions was a slow rate of fire using separate charges and shells. This was remedied by the time the IS-3 entered production. Symbolically, Josef Stalin tanks were at the head of the advance to Berlin in 1945 and remained in production after the war, being the world's most powerful tank for well over a decade.

Centurion

Development of the Centurion main battle tank was initiated in 1943, in response to a War Office requirement for a new heavy cruiser tank. A principal requirement was that it be able to withstand a direct hit from a 3.46 in (88 mm) gun.

COUNTRY OF ORIGIN: United Kingdom

CREW: 4

WEIGHT: 113,792 lb (51,723 kg)

DIMENSIONS: length 32 ft 4 in (9.854 m); width 11 ft 1.5 in (3.39 m); height 9 ft 10.5 in (3.009 m)

RANGE: 127 miles (205 km)

ARMOR: 2–6 in (51–152 mm)

ARMAMENT: one 4.13 in (105 mm) gun; two 0.30 in (7.62 mm) machine guns; one 0.50 in (12.7 mm) machine gun

POWERPLANT: Rolls-Royce Meteor Mk IVB V-12 petrol, developing 650 hp (485 kW)

PERFORMANCE: maximum road speed 43km/h (27mph); fording 1.45m (4ft 9in); vertical obstacle 0.91m (3ft); trench 3.352m (11ft)

The Centurion main battle tank incorporated all the lessons learned in the design of earlier generations of British tanks.

The Centurion main battle tank had its origins in World War II, when it was developed as a cruiser tank. The first prototype appeared in 1945 and the tank entered production shortly after.

A heavier version needed

At an early stage of the development program it was realized that the planned 40-ton (40,642 kg) design would have to be increased if this requirement was to be fulfilled, so work proceeded on a heavier version. By this time, construction of the first 40-ton (40,642 kg) prototypes was well advanced, and these were completed as the Centurion

Mk I. Only a few of these were produced before production switched to the more heavily armored Centurion Mk II. The Centurion saw action in Korea, Vietnam, Pakistan and the Middle East. Nearly 4500 were built before production ceased in 1962 and it was replaced by the Chieftain. However, its excellent capacity for upgrading ensured that it has remained in service beyond the 1960s with foreign armies. Among the many variants are an armored recovery vehicle (as well as an amphibious recovery vehicle which was used in the Falklands conflict in 1982), a bridge-layer and an AVRE. It is considered one of the most successful tank designs in the history of warfare.

The Centurion was hugely successful, thousands being built for service with armies all over the world, and many tank guns of today are based on its renowned L7 4.13 in (105 mm) weapon.

T-54/55

No other tank in the world was produced in such quantity as the T-54/55 series. It entered service as the Soviet Union's main battle tank in 1947 and was still serving in some countries 60 years later.

COUNTRY OF ORIGIN: USSR

CREW: 4

WEIGHT: 79,000 lb (35,909 kg)

DIMENSIONS: length 29 ft 6.3 in (9 m); width 10 ft 8.75 in (3.27 m); height 7 ft 10.5 in (2.4 m)

RANGE: 249 miles (400 km)

ARMOR: 0.79–9.84 in (20–250 mm)

ARMAMENT: one 3.94 in (100 mm) gun; two 0.30 in (7.62 mm) machine guns (one coaxial, one in bow); one 0.50 in (12.7 mm) anti-aircraft machine gun

POWERPLANT: one V-12 diesel engine developing 520 hp (388 kW)

PERFORMANCE: maximum road speed 30 mph (48 km/h); fording 4 ft 7 in (1.4 m); vertical obstacle 2 ft 7.5 in (0.8 m); trench 8 ft 10.25 in (2.7 m)

A Chinese T-54 with the turret traversed to the rear, and the loader mannning the 0.50 in (12.7 mm) DshKM anti-aircraft machine gun.

The prototype of the T-54 was completed in 1946 and production began some years later. The T-54 and its variants were built in larger numbers than any other Soviet tank after World War II (around 50,000), also being produced in Czechoslovakia, Poland and China. The T-54 was continually updated prior to the arrival of the T-55, with gun-stabilizers and an infrared capability added.

Extensive combat

Variants included flame-throwers, dozers, bridge-layers, mine-clearers, recovery vehicles and a combat engineer vehicle. The tank saw extensive combat in Angola, North Africa, the Far East and in particular the Middle East, where it suffered by comparison to Israeli Centurion and M48 tanks during the Arab-Israeli wars. During the Six Day War of 1967 and the Yom Kippur War of 1973 Israel captured over 1000 T-54/55s and retained many of them for service in the Israeli Army, replacing the Soviet 3.94 in (100 mm) gun with a 4.13 in (105 mm) L5 or M68 and the Russian engine with a General Motors diesel. In Israeli service the T-54/55 was known as the Tiran-5. After their retirement from reserve units in the 1990s many were sold to Latin American countries, while others were modified as armored personnel carriers.

Simple and produced in mass numbers, the T-54/55's main armament was originally the D-10T 3.94 in (100 mm) rifled gun, a very large caliber weapon for its time but long since made obsolete by its inability to penetrate modern armor with the types of ammunition it used.

M48A3 Patton

The M48 was the second of the "General Patton" series of tanks, the first being the M47. The M48 was a successful design from the outset, and went on to perform well in conflicts around the world.

An M48 advancing during street fighting in Saigon, Vietnam, in May 1968.

COUNTRY OF ORIGIN: United States

CREW: 4

WEIGHT: 103,488 lb (47,040 kg)

DIMENSIONS: length 28 ft 6 in (8.6 m); width 11 ft 11 in (3.6 m); height 10 ft 3 in (3.2 m)

RANGE: 288 miles (463 km)

ARMOR: 0.5–4.72 in (12.7–120 mm)

ARMAMENT: one 3.54 in (90 mm) gun; one 0.30 in (7.62 mm) coaxial machine gun; one 0.50 in (12.7 mm) machine gun in commander's cupola

POWERPLANT: one Continental AVDS-1790-2A 12-cylinder diesel engine developing 750 hp (560 kW)

PERFORMANCE: maximum road speed 30 mph (48.2 km/h); fording 4 ft (1.219 m); vertical obstacle 3 ft (0.915 m); trench 8 ft 6 in (2.59 m)

When the Korean War began, the US military had no medium tanks in production. The M47 was an interim measure but work instantly began on the M48. The first "Pattons" were ready in July 1952. The speed of development resulted in teething troubles for the early Pattons, including poor reliability and a short operating range. The A3 was a highly modified version designed to rectify these failings, and the M48 served successfully in Vietnam, India and with the Israelis in the Middle East.

Infantry support role

The M48 has been used as the basis for flame-thrower tanks, recovery vehicles and an AVLB. The A5 was an upgraded version produced in the mid-1970s which extended the M48's shelf-life considerably, and it is still being used in some countries today. The M48 was used in the infantry support role in combat during the Vietnam War. It was first used in tank-versus-tank combat during the Indo-Pakistan war of 1965, where it suffered heavy losses. At the Battle of Asal Uttar, during an assault on Indian positions, the Pakistanis lost 100 M48s, although losses decreased after the Pakistanis revised their tactics.

The M48 was very effective in American hands, but less so in the service of other armies whose tactics left much to be desired. It was out-fought by the British-built Centurion.

M103 Heavy Tank

The American M103 heavy tank was designed as a counter to heavy Soviet AFVs like the IS and T-10. It was never used in action and its size and weight made operations difficult.

COUNTRY OF ORIGIN: United States	
CREW: 5	
WEIGHT: 124,544 lb (56,610 kg)	
DIMENSIONS: length 37 ft 1.5 in (11.3 m); width 12 ft 4 in (3.8 m); height 9 ft 5.3 in (2.9 m)	
RANGE: 80 miles (130 km)	
ARMOR: 0.5–7 in (12.7–178 mm)	
ARMAMENT: one 4.72 in (120 mm) rifled gun; one 0.30 in (7.62 mm) coaxial machine gun; one 0.50 in (12.7 mm) anti-aircraft machine gun	
POWERPLANT: one Continental AV-1790-5B or 7C V-12 petrol engine developing 810 hp (604 kW)	
PERFORMANCE: maximum road speed 21 mph (34 km/h); vertical obstacle 3 ft (0.91 m); trench 7 ft 6 in (2.29 m)	

One of the M-103 prototypes pictured with its turret traversed to the rear and the gun travel lock open.

The advent of the Cold War saw the US begin work on a new tank designed for direct assault and long-range anti-tank support for medium tanks against Soviet armor. Early prototypes of the M103 showed deficiencies in both the turret and gun control equipment. Despite modifications, the 200 built by Chrysler for deployment in Europe proved difficult to use because of their size (which made concealment difficult), weight and small range, as well as poor reliability. They were phased out during the 1960s. Their bulk required a specialized recovery vehicle, built on the M103's chassis and named the M51. Nevertheless, the M103 was part of a trend for bigger and more heavily armed tanks on NATO's front line.

An enlarged turret

The successive versions of the M103 shared many components with the M47, M48 and M60, although the turret was larger to accommodate the massive 4.72 in (120 mm) gun, its two loaders, the gunner and commander. The number of M103s in service was reduced during the 1960s and the last examples were withdrawn in 1974.

The M103's powerful rifled 4.73 in (120 mm) gun was designed to penetrate the armor of the heaviest Soviet tanks, which existing NATO tank guns were unable to do.

PT-76

Although production of the PT-76 ended in 1963, the tank continues in use with armies that were once allied to the former Warsaw Pact, and has seen much action in various parts of the world.

COUNTRY OF ORIGIN: USSR

CREW: 3

WEIGHT: 30,800 lb (14,000 kg)

DIMENSIONS: length 25 ft 0.25 in (7.625 m); width 10 ft 3.7 in (3.14 m); height 7 ft 4.75 in (2.255 m)

RANGE: 160 miles (260 km)

ARMOR: 0.19–0.66 in (5–17 mm)

ARMAMENT: one 2.99 in (76 mm) gun; one coaxial 0.30 in (7.62 mm) machine gun; one 0.50 in (12.7 mm) anti-aircraft machine-gun

POWERPLANT: one V-6 six-cylinder diesel engine developing 240 hp (179 kW)

PERFORMANCE: maximum road speed 27 mph (44 km/h); fording amphibious; vertical obstacle 3 ft 7.3 in (1.10 m); trench 9 ft 2 in (2.8 m)

A PT-76 is photographed rolling from a Soviet landing craft during an amphibious warfare exercise.

The PT-76 was designed immediately after World War II. For years it was the standard reconnaissance vehicle of the Soviet Red Army, before being replaced by heavier T-62s, and was exported to more than 25 countries, seeing action in the 1967 Six Day War, Vietnam and Angola. Intended as an amphibious tank, its armor could only withstand small-arms fire, to keep the weight down. The tank was equipped with bilge pumps and water jets to allow it to move through water and could travel up to 40 miles (65 km) in this way. The chassis was used for a number of other vehicles, including the BTR-50 Armored Personnel Carrier and the FROG missile launcher. Development of the PT-76 began in 1949, and the type was accepted for service in 1952. Production started in 1953 at the Stalingrad (later Volgograd) Tank Factory.

Swimming tank

The designation PT-76 is an abbreviation of Plavayushchy Tank (literally swimming tank). About 7000 PT-76s were built before production ended in 1963, 2000 vehicles being exported to 24 countries within the Soviet sphere of influence. The production total includes an improved variant, the PT-76B, which appeared in 1958.

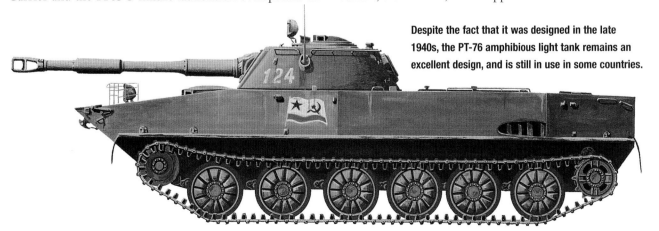

Despite the fact that it was designed in the late 1940s, the PT-76 amphibious light tank remains an excellent design, and is still in use in some countries.

AMX-13

The AMX-13 was France's first post-war light tank design and was a huge success, being widely exported to 24 countries as well as serving with the French Army.

The AMX-13 was one of three armored vehicles designed in France immediately after the end of World War II.

COUNTRY OF ORIGIN: France

CREW: 3

WEIGHT: 33,000 lb (15,000 kg)

DIMENSIONS: length 20 ft 10.3 in (6.36 m); width 8 ft 2.5 in (2.50 m); height 7 ft 6.5 in (2.30 m)

RANGE: 250 miles (400 km)

ARMOR: 0.4–1.57 in (10–40 mm)

ARMAMENT: one 2.95 in (75 mm) gun; one 0.30 in (7.62 mm) machine gun

POWERPLANT: one SOFAM eight-cylinder petrol engine developing 250 hp (186 kW)

PERFORMANCE: maximum road speed 37 mph (60 km/h); fording 1 ft 11.7 in (0.60 m); vertical obstacle 2 ft 1.7 in (0.65 m); trench 5 ft 3 in (1.60 m)

The AMX-13 was designed immediately after the end of World War II. Production began in 1952 and continued until the 1980s. Its design included an automatic loader in the turret bustle. This had two revolver-type magazines, each holding six rounds of ammunition.

Oscillating turret feature

The tank was widely exported, proving particularly popular with developing nations. The AMX-13 was phased out of service with the French Army in the 1970s, but the vehicle was exported to 24 countries, and continues to serve with some of these. The biggest export customer was Singapore, which purchased 350 units. Some of the export variants are armed with a 4.13 in (105 mm) gun. The AMX-13 saw action with the Israeli Army in the Six Day War of 1967, but this version's 2.95 in (75 mm) gun was ineffective against the armor of the T-54 and T-55 main battle tanks used by Egypt and Syria, so the tank was phased out, some going to Singapore. One interesting feature is the oscillating turret in which the gun is fixed in the upper part, which in turn pivots on the lower part. The AMX-13 was extensively modified and used as the basis for a complete family of vehicles, from self-propelled guns and howitzers to engineer vehicles, recovery vehicles, bridge-layers and infantry fighting vehicles.

Later versions of the AMX were armed with a 3.54 in (90 mm) or 4.13 in (105 mm) gun, the latter pictured here. French tank designers got it exactly right with this vehicle, as its remarkable export sales proved.

T-10

Developed in the late 1940s, the T-10 became operational in 1955. The tank remained in production until 1966, when the USSR dispensed with its heavy tanks, although some served until 1993.

COUNTRY OF ORIGIN: USSR

CREW: 4

WEIGHT: 109,760 lb (49,890 kg)

DIMENSIONS: length (including gun) 32 ft 4.75 in (9.875 m); length (hull) 23 ft 1 in (7.04 m); width 11 ft 8.5 in (3.566 m); height 7 ft 4.5 in (2.25 m)

RANGE: 155 miles (250 km)

ARMOR: 0.79–9.84 in (20–250 mm)

ARMAMENT: one 4.8 in (122 mm) gun; two 0.50 in (12.7 mm) machine guns (one coaxial, one anti-aircraft)

POWERPLANT: one V-12 diesel engine developing 700 hp (522 kW)

PERFORMANCE: maximum road speed 26 mph (42 km/h); vertical obstacle 35.5 in (0.9 m); trench 9 ft 10 in (3.0 m)

The Soviet Union continued to develop heavy tanks after the end of World War II, the massive T-10 being the last of the line.

The T-10 was developed in the USSR after the end of World War II. At least 2500 were built up to the late 1950s. It was designed to provide long-range fire-support for the T-54/55s, and act as a spearhead for thrusts through heavily defended areas. Its cramped confines required the use of separate-loading ammunition as there was no room for complete shells. The T-10A and T-10B were improved models, the former having two-axis gun stabilization and the latter improved gunnery optics. About 2500 examples of all models were built before production ended in 1966. In addition to the Soviet Army, the T-10 was used by Egypt, North Vietnam and Syria. The final version was the T-10M, which was equipped with a longer M-62-T2 (L/43) gun with five-baffle muzzle brake, a two-axis

gun stabilizer, heavier caliber machine guns, infrared night vision equipment and NBC protection.

Decrease in speed

After leaving front-line service it was kept in reserve for many years. The decrease in speed compared to the earlier T-34 was surprising given the Red Army's emphasis on speed and mass during and after World War II. The Soviets certainly possessed mass, but vehicles such as the T-10 reduced overall speed.

A T-10 heavy tank with a 0.50 in (12.7 mm) DshKM heavy anti-aircraft machine gun mounted on the commander's cupola. The T-10 was armed with a 4.8 in (122 mm) gun. Some former Egyptian T-10s were used by Israel for static defense on the Suez Canal.

M50 Ontos

Developed as a light, air-transportable anti-tank missile system intended for rapid overseas deployment, the M50 was an ugly vehicle nicknamed Ontos, meaning "The Thing" in Greek.

COUNTRY OF ORIGIN: United States	
CREW: 3	
WEIGHT: 19,051 lb (8640 kg)	
DIMENSIONS: Length: 12.53 ft (3.82 m); width: 8.53 ft (2.6 m); height: 6.99 ft (2.13 m)	
RANGE: 150 miles (240 km)	
ARMOR: 0.51 in (13 mm) maximum	
ARMAMENT: six x RCL 4.17 in (106 mm) recoilless rifles; 4 x 0.5 in (12.7 mm) M8C spotting rifles	
POWERPLANT: one 6-cylinder General Motors 302 petrol, developing 145 hp (108 kW)	
PERFORMANCE: maximum road speed 30 mph (48 km/h)	

Surely one of the ugliest AFVs ever to appear, the Ontos was subjected to intensive trials just before the US Army cancelled its order.

The M50 Ontos was a tank destroyer designed for use as an air-portable vehicle for the US Marine Corps. Its chassis was developed in the early 1950s by GMC, and its weaponry consisted of six RCL 4.17 in (106 mm) recoilless rifles, three mounted either side of a small central turret. Attached to the top four guns were 0.5 in (12.7 mm) spotting rifles. Six 4.17 in (106 mm) rounds were pre-loaded and a further eight were kept inside the vehicle. A major disadvantage of the M50 was that the rifles could only be reloaded from the outside, thus exposing the crew to small arms fire. The prototype, built by Allis–Chalmers in 1952, was based on the chassis of the M56 Scorpion light anti-tank vehicle.

Cancelled orders

Exhaustive trials were carried out, and almost as soon as these were completed in 1955 the US Army cancelled its order. The US Marine Corps, however, ordered 297. The first vehicle was delivered in October 1956 and production was completed in 1957. Ontos was extensively used by the USMC in Vietnam as a fire support vehicle.

Although the M50 proved quite useful as a fire support vehicle in Vietnam, it would have been much less effective against a full-scale Soviet armored assault in Europe. After service in Vietnam, the survivors were shipped back to the USA and scrapped.

Conqueror

Together with the US M103, the British Conqueror tank was intended to combat Soviet heavy armor like the IS-3, and was armed with a powerful 4.72 in (120 mm) main gun. Its main problem was that its weight made it unwieldy.

The Conqueror originated in a heavy tank requirement issued in 1944. It was intended to work alongside the Churchill.

COUNTRY OF ORIGIN: United Kingdom	
CREW: 4	
WEIGHT: 142,688 lb (64,858 kg)	
DIMENSIONS: length (gun forwards) 38 ft (11.58 m); length (hull) 25 ft 4 in (7.72 m); width 13 ft 1 in (3.99 m); height 11 ft (3.35 m)	
RANGE: 95 miles (155 km)	
ARMOR: 0.66–7 in (17–178 mm)	
ARMAMENT: one 4.72 in (120 mm) rifled gun; one 0.30 in (7.62 mm) coaxial machine gun	
POWERPLANT: one 12-cylinder petrol engine developing 810 hp (604 kW)	
PERFORMANCE: maximum road speed 21.3 mph (34 km/h); vertical obstacle 3 ft (0.91 m); trench 11 ft (3.35 m)	

The FV214 Conqueror was a post-war heavy tank for the British Army to use in the expected massed armored clash with the tanks of the Warsaw Pact on the central European plain. The British were determined that the experience of 1940, when their tanks had been out-gunned by the German panzers, would not happen again.

Problems emerge

Based on the Centurion, nearly 200 Conquerors were built between 1955 and 1958, mostly deployed in support of Centurion squadrons in the British Army of the Rhine.

It was then that problems began to reveal themselves. The Conqueror possessed very heavy armor – it was 7 in (178 mm) thick at the front – and this contributed to the tank being overweight, as did the large turret, fitted with a rotating cupola for the commander. All this made the tank cumbersome and difficult to maintain. Its advantage over the Centurion was its longer-range gun, so when the Centurion was upgunned there was no longer a role for the Conqueror. It was phased out in the 1960s.

The Conqueror heavy tank was produced to counter the threat posed by the USSR's IS-3. In service, it proved ponderous and lacked the mobility essential for rapid deployment in the face of an enemy armored attack.

M60A3

The M60A3 incorporated a number of technological advances such as a new rangefinder and ballistic computer and a turret stabilization system. All American M60s were upgraded to this standard.

COUNTRY OF ORIGIN: United States	
CREW: 4	
WEIGHT: 107,520 lb (48,872 kg)	
DIMENSIONS: length 30 ft 11.5 in (9.436 m); width 11 ft 11 in (3.631 m); height 10 ft 8.25 in (3.27 m)	
RANGE: 310 miles (500 km)	
ARMOR: 0.98–5 in (25–127 mm)	
ARMAMENT: one 4.13 in (105 mm) gun; one 0.50 in (12.7 mm) machine gun; one 0.30 in (7.62 mm) coaxial machine gun	
POWERPLANT: one Continental 12-cylinder diesel engine developing 750 hp (560 kW)	
PERFORMANCE: maximum road speed 30 mph (48.28 km/h); fording 4 ft (1.219 m); vertical obstacle 3 ft (0.914 m); trench 8 ft 6 in (2.59 m)	

The M60's gun was fitted with a thermal sleeve, designed to prolong the useful life of the barrel before it needed to be changed.

The development of the US M60 series of tanks began in 1956 to create an improved M48. Built by General Dynamics, it entered service in 1960, but was superseded by the A1 to A3 versions. The A3 is notable for its laser fire-control system and thermal sights. The two main variants are an AVLB and a Combat Engineer Vehicle, armed with a demolition charge and dozer blade. The M60A3 has been widely exported to Austria, Italy (where it was built under license), North Africa and many Middle East countries. It is still in service in Africa and the Middle East, particularly in Turkey and Israel, while in the USA its bridge-layer version remains in National Guard use.

Effective against Iraqi armor

The M60 first saw combat during the Arab-Israeli Yom Kippur War of October 1973, and in the invasion of Lebanon in 1982. M60s operating with the US Marine Corps and the Royal Saudi Army also saw combat in Operation Desert Storm in 1991, where they led the attack on Iraqi forces in Kuwait and subsequently spearheaded the drive to Kuwait City. It proved effective against all types of Iraqi armor, including the T-62, which it had been developed to counter many years earlier.

The M60 has proved to be one of the world's most successful main battle tanks, and has seen service with some 20 armies since it was first deployed in 1960. It was used in large numbers during the Gulf War of 1991.

SPz lang HS30

The Schützenpanzer lang HS30 armored personnel carrier was built to a Swiss design, developed by Hispano-Suiza and powered by an 8-cylinder Rolls-Royce engine.

COUNTRY OF ORIGIN: West Germany

CREW: 3–5

WEIGHT: 32,200 lb (14,600 kg)

DIMENSIONS: Length: 18.24 ft (5.56 m); width: 7.38 ft (2.25 m); height: 6.07 ft (1.85 m)

RANGE: 170 miles (270 km)

ARMOR: (Steel) 1.18 in (30 mm) maximum

ARMAMENT: one x 0.78 in (20 mm) Hispano HS820 cannon and other options

POWERPLANT: one x Rolls-Royce 8-cylinder petrol, developing 235 hp (175 kW) at 3800 rpm

PERFORMANCE: maximum road speed 32 mph (51 km/h); fording 2.3 ft (0.7 m); gradient 60 percent; vertical obstacle 2 ft (0.6 m); trench 5.3 ft (1.6 m)

The HS30 was quite useless as an infantry combat vehicle, and became the subject of a scandal. This example is armed with 4.17 in (106 mm) recoilless rifles.

The HS30 was destined to be blighted by technical problems throughout its active life, and only 2176 vehicles were built (out of a projected 4450) between 1958 and 1962. In the early 1970s, remaining HS30s were replaced with Marder mechanized infantry combat vehicles.

Serious deficits

The HS30 was a basic armored personnel carrier that could carry five soldiers and a three-man crew inside an all-welded steel hull. It was not amphibious, neither did it have an NBC option, both serious deficits in the Cold War era. It was, however, well armed. A turret-mounted 0.78 in (20 mm) Hispano HS820 was the primary weapon, but ATGWs and M40A1 4.17 in (106 mm) recoilless rifles were further options; however the back blast from a recoilless rifle would quickly give the vehicle's position away. The ineffective HS30 is perhaps best remembered for its key role in a major political scandal in the early 1960s, when a leading German news magazine accused the then Federal German Defense Minister of bribery and highlighted critical deficiencies in the Bundeswehr's state of preparedness faced with the threat from the east.

Although it appeared a formidable enough weapon, the HS30 lacked all the attributes of a modern armored personnel carrier, such as NBC protection and an amphibious capability.

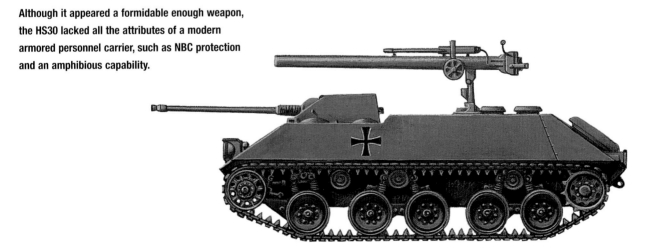

Type 59

China's Type 59 main battle tank was a direct copy of the Russian T-54, and formed the bulk of the Chinese People's Liberation Army's armored strength for decades.

COUNTRY OF ORIGIN: China

CREW: 4

WEIGHT: 79,200 lb (36,000 kg)

DIMENSIONS: length 27 ft 6 in (9 m); width 10 ft (3.27 m); height 7 ft 8 in (2.59 m)

RANGE: 375 miles (600 km)

ARMOR: 1.5–8 in (39–203 mm)

ARMAMENT: one 3.94 in (100 mm) gun; two 0.30 in (7.62 mm) machine guns; one 0.50 in (12.7 mm) machine gun

POWERPLANT: one Model 12150L V-12 diesel engine developing 520 hp (388 kW)

PERFORMANCE: maximum road speed: 31.3 mph (50 km/h); fording 4 ft 7 in (1.4 m); vertical obstacle 2 ft 7 in (0.79 m); trench 8 ft 10 in (2.7 m)

Type 59 main battle tanks on parade. The Type 59 is essentially a refined Soviet T-54.

The Type 59 was a Chinese version of the T-54 which had been supplied by the USSR in the early 1950s. The first Chinese-assembled T-54A, using kits from the USSR, was rolled out in 1958. Small numbers of T-54As built with Chinese components were being produced by 1959, the vehicle being designated Type 59. Series production of the Type 59 began in 1963, and 10,000 units in a number of variants were built before the production finally ceased in the late 1980s. Early models were very basic, with no gun stabilization or infrared night-vision equipment, though the latter was supplied to later models by the British company MEL. A laser rangefinder was also added later,

but it was mounted on the front of the turret, where it was vulnerable to shell splinters and small-arms fire.

Accidentally arming the enemy

The tank can generate its own smoke screen by injecting diesel fuel into the exhaust pipe, and extra fuel can be mounted in drums on the rear hull. The Type 59 was exported in some quantity to Albania, the Congo, North Korea, Pakistan, Sudan and Vietnam, the latter proving an unwise choice given the subsequent war between China and Vietnam in 1979.

China's Type 59 main battle tank captured the world's headlines in 1989, when it was used against student demonstrators in Beijing's Tiananmen Square. The picture of a lone student confronting one became a classic image of the twentieth century.

M551 Sheridan

The Sheridan light tank had a poor operational record, and was only retained in service because of its air-portable capability. Some were used in the US invasion of Panama in 1989.

COUNTRY OF ORIGIN: United States

CREW: 4

WEIGHT: 3,482 lb (15,830 kg)

DIMENSIONS: length 20 ft 8 in (6.299 m); width 9 ft 3 in (2.819 m); height 9 ft 8 in (2.946 m)

RANGE: 310 miles (600 km)

ARMOR: 1.57–2 in (40–50 mm)

ARMAMENT: one 5.98 in (152 mm) gun/missile launcher; one coaxial 0.30 in (7.62 mm) machine gun; one 0.50 in (12.7 mm) anti-aircraft machine gun

POWERPLANT: one six-cylinder Detroit 6V-53T diesel, developing 300 hp (224 kW)

PERFORMANCE: maximum road speed 43 mph (70 km/h); fording: amphibious; vertical obstacle 2 ft 9 in (0.838 m); trench 8 ft 4 in (2.54 m)

After its operational days were over the Sheridan continued to fulfill an important training role, with some being converted to resemble Soviet AFVs.

In 1959, the US Army wanted a new air-portable light tank to replace the M41 light tank and the M56 self-propelled gun in service with the US airborne forces, so a new vehicle was developed under the name Armored Reconnaissance/Airborne Assault Vehicle (AR/AAV) and was designated XM551. The contract was awarded to the Allison Division of General Motors, which produced 12 prototypes. Evaluation of these was still incomplete in 1965, when the company was awarded a four-year production contract. The vehicle was accepted for service in 1966 and given the name M551 General Sheridan, after Civil War General Philip Sheridan, and deployed with the US Army to Europe, South Korea and Vietnam.

Light all-round armor

Between 1966 and 1970, 1700 Sheridans were built. Several faults were found, mostly in operation in Vietnam, where the vehicle proved vulnerable to mines because of its light belly armor. In fact, the armor was light all round, and could be penetrated by heavy machine gun rounds. Some Sheridans were equipped to carry the Shillelagh gun-launched anti-tank missile, but it was found that the firing of the 5.98 in (152 mm) gun upset the missile's circuitry. The Sheridan was withdrawn from first-line service in the 1980s except with a battalion of the 82nd Airborne Division, which used it until the mid-1990s.

An M551 Sheridan, as deployed in Vietnam, features extensive turret stowage and extra protection for the commander.

T-62

The T-62 was innovative in that it mounted the world's first smooth-bore tank gun, but it proved something of a disaster in combat, being poorly armored and prone to catching fire.

COUNTRY OF ORIGIN: USSR

CREW: 4

WEIGHT: 87,808 lb (39,912 kg)

DIMENSIONS: length 28 ft 6 in (9.34 m); width 10 ft 1 in (3.3 m); height: 7 ft 5 in (2.4 m)

RANGE: 406 miles (650 km)

ARMOR: 0.59–9.52 in (15–242 mm)

ARMAMENT: one 4.53 in (115 mm) U-5TS gun; one 0.30 in (7.62 mm) coaxial machine gun

POWERPLANT: one V-55-5 V-12 liquid-cooled diesel, developing 580 hp (432 kW)

PERFORMANCE: maximum road speed 37.5 mph (60 km/h); fording 4 ft 7 in (1.4 m); vertical obstacle 2 ft 7.5 in (0.8 m); trench 8 ft 10.25 in (2.7 m)

The angle to which the T-62's gun can be depressed is slightly more than that of the T-54/55 series, giving a better hull-down firing position.

The Russian T-62 was a development of the T-54/55 series, but due to the cost of each tank, it never replaced its predecessor, which outlived it in production. Built from 1961 until the early 1970s, the T-62 had an unusual integral shell-case ejection system. The recoil of the gun ejected the case out of a trapdoor in the turret, saving space but reducing the overall rate of fire. Able to deep-ford by means of a snorkel over the loader's hatch, the tank was fitted with infrared night-vision equipment; turret-ventilation system; nuclear, biological and chemical (NBC) protection; and the ability to create an instant smoke screen by injecting diesel into the exhaust.

The T-62 had its combat debut during the Yom Kippur War of 1973, when it revealed an unpleasant tendency to catch fire when penetrated.

Captured by the Israelis

The Israelis captured several hundred from the Egyptians and Syrians and pressed them into service, adding thermal-imaging equipment and laser rangefinders, improving the armor and replacing the unreliable Soviet diesel engines with reliable American ones. In Israeli service the T-62 was known as the Tiran-6.

The T-62 was widely used during the decade of Soviet operations in Afghanistan. It suffered heavily in action against Israeli M60s during the 1973 Yom Kippur War.

Chieftain Mk 5

Together with Germany's Leopard, the British Chieftain would have borne the brunt of any tank battle that might have developed on the North German plain, and have played a decisive part in blunting any Soviet offensive.

Until the introduction of Germany's Leopard 2, the Chieftain was the best-protected and most powerful of all NATO's main battle tanks.

The Chieftain was designed in the late 1950s as a successor to the Centurion. Production began in 1963. Over 900 entered service with the British Army, with considerable numbers being sold to Kuwait and Iran.

Iran–Iraq combat

The largest export order came from Iran (707 ordered), including bridge-laying and recovery versions, in addition to a further 187 upgraded and improved Chieftains. The Iranian Chieftains saw combat in the Iran–Iraq war during the 1980s. Jordan also received 274 Chieftains. Until the

Leopard 2 entered German service in 1980, the Chieftain was the best-armed and -armored main battle tank in the world, and was the mainstay of UK armored forces on NATO's front line in Germany, with frequent additions such as laser-rangefinders and thermal-imaging devices, until being slowly replaced by the Challenger in the late 1980s. It included a bridge-layer, engineer tank and recovery vehicle among its variants. The Chieftains in British Army service are now in reserve.

COUNTRY OF ORIGIN: United Kingdom	
CREW: 4	
WEIGHT: 120,736 lb (54,880 kg)	
DIMENSIONS: length (with gun forward) 35 ft 5 in (10.795 m); length (hull) 24 ft 8 in (7.518 m); width 11 ft 8.5 in (3.657 m); height (overall) 9 ft 6 in (2.895 m)	
RANGE: 310 miles (500 km)	
ARMOR: classified	
ARMAMENT: one 4.72 in (120 mm) rifled gun; one 0.30 in (7.62 mm) coaxial machine gun; six smoke dischargers	
POWERPLANT: one Leyland six-cylinder multi-fuel engine developing 750 hp (560 kW)	
PERFORMANCE: maximum road speed 30 mph (48 km/h); fording 3 ft 6 in (1.066 m); vertical obstacle 3 ft (0.914 m); trench 10 ft 4 in (3.149 m)	

A Chieftain main battle tank armed with a 4.72 in (120 mm) L11A5 rifled tank gun. The latter is fitted with a thermal sleeve to reduce barrel distortion and prolong its useful life before a change is needed.

Leopard I

The Leopard I main battle tank was a key element of NATO's land warfare defense during the most dangerous years of the Cold War. It was originally intended to be a joint Franco-German collaborative project.

COUNTRY OF ORIGIN: West Germany	
CREW: 4	
WEIGHT: 87,808 lb (39,912 kg)	
DIMENSIONS: length (with gun forward) 31 ft 4 in (9.543 m); length (hull) 23 ft 3 in (7.09 m); width 10 ft 8 in (3.25 m); height (overall) 8 ft 7 in (2.613 m)	
RANGE: 373 miles (600 km)	
ARMOR: classified	
ARMAMENT: one 4.13 in (105 mm) gun; one coaxial 0.30 in (7.62 mm) machine gun; 0.30 in (7.62 mm) anti-aircraft machine gun; four smoke dischargers	
POWERPLANT: one MTU 10-cylinder diesel engine developing 830 hp (619 kW)	
PERFORMANCE: maximum road speed 40.4 mph (65 km/h); fording 7 ft 4 in (2.25 m); vertical obstacle 3 ft 9.25 in (1.15 m); trench 9 ft 10 in (3 m)	

By the standards of its day, the Leopard 1 was a capable main battle tank offering a high level of agility and firepower.

Germany's design for the intended 1960s Franco-German joint venture was the Leopard 1 and the Germans eventually adopted it independently of the French. Testing of the various prototypes began in 1960. Porsche's design was selected, although some changes were made before it was accepted for production. These included a new cast turret and several hull changes to raise the rear deck in order to make a roomier engine compartment. An optical rangefinder system was also added. Built by Krauss-Maffei,

the first production vehicles appeared in 1965 and production continued until 1979, a total of 2237 being built for the German Army and many more for export.

Four basic versions

There were four basic versions, differing in armor, turret-type and fire-control systems. The tank formed the basis of a complete family of vehicles designed to support the vehicle on the battlefield. Optional equipment for the tank included a snorkel for deep-wading and a hydraulic blade to be attached to the front. The Leopard 1 was undoubtedly one of the best tanks designs to have come out of Europe, but is now outdated.

When it was first deployed as part of NATO's front line, the Leopard 1 was a very capable main battle tank offering a high level of agility and excellent firepower, thanks to its 4.13 in (105 mm) L7 gun of British design.

AMX-30

One of the most successful of France's modern armored fighting vehicle designs, France's AMX-30 main battle tank has been exported to a dozen countries, with Spain the first customer.

COUNTRY OF ORIGIN: France

CREW: 4

WEIGHT: 79,072 lb (35,941 kg)

DIMENSIONS: length (with gun forward) 31 ft 1 in (9.48 m); length (hull) 21 ft 7 in (6.59 m); width 10 ft 2 in (3.1 m); height (overall) 9 ft 4 in (2.86 m)

RANGE: 373 miles (600 km)

ARMOR: 0.6–3.1 in (15–80 mm)

ARMAMENT: one 4.13 in (105 mm) gun; one coaxial 0.78 in (20 mm) cannon; one 0.30 in (7.62 mm) machine gun

POWERPLANT: one Hispano-Suiza 12-cylinder diesel, developing 720hp (537kW)

PERFORMANCE: maximum road speed 40 mph (65 km/h); vertical obstacle 3 ft 0.6 in (0.93 m); trench 9 ft 6 in (2.9 m)

The AMX-30 was not fitted with a main armament stabilizing system, so could not fire accurately on the move.

Until the mid-1950s, both France and Germany relied on American M47s for their armor, though France also had a number of the excellent German Panther tanks. A requirement was drawn up for a new main battle tank, lighter and more powerfully armed than the M47, to supply both countries. However, typically, each adopted their own design. The French produced the AMX-30, the first production tanks appearing in 1966, half of which were destined for export.

Action in the Gulf War
The French Army took delivery of 387 AMX-30s and 659 AMX-30B2s, the latter introducing a number of improvements including an integrated fire-control system incorporating a laser rangefinder and a low-light TV system, and an upgraded automotive system including a new transmission. The AMX-30 was used in action during the Gulf War of 1991, where it operated in support of the 6th Light Armored Division on the left flank of the Coalition invasion. The AMX-30 chassis has been used for a number of other vehicles including the Pluton tactical nuclear missile launcher, as well as a self-propelled anti-aircraft gun, a recovery vehicle, bridge-layer and engineer vehicles. The tank has seen service with the Iraqi, Saudi Arabian and Spanish armies in addition to the French.

The primary anti-tank round of the AMX-30's 4.13 in (105 mm) gun is the OCC (HEAT) type, which has the ability to penetrate 15.75 in (400 mm) of armor and has a muzzle velocity of 3280 ft (1000 m) per second.

Stridsvagn 103 (S-tank)

Developed by Bofors, the Stridsvagn Strv 103 S-Tank had its origins in a requirement by the Swedish Army to replace its fleet of 300 Centurions, as well as other armored fighting vehicles, with a home-grown battle tank.

Without a turret the S-tank had a very low hull silhouette, but the front of the hull had to be raised to elevate the gun.

COUNTRY OF ORIGIN: Sweden
CREW: 3
WEIGHT: 85,568 lb (38,894 kg)
DIMENSIONS: length (with gun) 29 ft 6 in (8.99 m); length (hull) 23 ft 1 in (7.04 m); width 10 ft 8.3 in (3.26 m); height (overall) 8 ft 2.5 in (2.5 m)
RANGE: 242 miles (390 km)
ARMOR: 3.54–3.94 in (90–100 mm)
ARMAMENT: one 4.13 in (105 mm) gun; three 0.30 in (7.62 mm) machine guns
POWERPLANT: one diesel engine developing 240 hp (119 kW) and a Boeing 553 gas turbine, developing 490 hp (366 kW)
PERFORMANCE: maximum road speed 31 mph (50 km/h); fording 4 ft 11 in (1.5 m); vertical obstacle 2 ft 11.5 in (0.9 m); trench 7 ft 6.5 in (2.3 m)

Just after World War II, Sweden's armored forces mainly consisted of light tanks, so work began on an indigenous heavy tank with the gun fixed to the chassis rather than a turret. Aiming was achieved by turning the vehicle and raising or lowering the suspension, a new concept. When the requirement was issued, a heavy tank, KRV, was under development, but this was abandoned and the emphasis switched to completing the Strv 103. The S-Tank was a veritable test-bed of novelties, the most obvious of which was the absence of a turret. This layout was adopted so that the tank could keep a low profile in action.

Stand still to fire

Its only real drawback was that it was unable to fire on the move, but as Sweden was only likely to be engaged in defensive actions, this was not too problematic. Bofors began production in 1966, and 300 were completed by the time they ceased in 1971. The tank included a dozer blade and a flotation screen for amphibious capability. The radical Swedish S-tank generated considerable foreign interest, but few export orders.

The Stridsvagn 103 S-Tank had a bold design concept. The box at the rear of the hull is for external stowage of equipment. Novel though it was, the S-Tank did not attract overseas customers.

Raketenjagdpanzer 2

Fast and maneuverable, the Raketenjagdpanzer 2 was an extremely important asset to NATO's European land forces, which had to contend with the prospect of a massive Soviet armored assault.

COUNTRY OF ORIGIN: West Germany
CREW: 4
WEIGHT: 50,700 lb (23,000 kg)
DIMENSIONS: Length 21.09 ft (6.43 m); width 9.78 ft (2.98 m); height 7.05 ft (2.15 m)
RANGE: 250 miles (400 km)
ARMOR: (Steel) 1.97 in (50 mm)
ARMAMENT: fourteen x SS-11 ATGWs; 2 x 0.3 in (7.62 mm) MG3 MGs
POWERPLANT: one x Daimler-Benz MB 837A 8-cylinder diesel, developing 500 hp (373 kW) at 2000rpm
PERFORMANCE: maximum road speed 43 mph (70 km/h); fording 4.6 ft (1.4 m); gradient 60 percent; vertical obstacle 2.46 ft (0.75 m); trench 6.6 ft (2 m)

Light and fast, the Raketenjagdpanzer 2 was ideally placed to ambush Soviet armor.

The Raketenjagdpanzer 2 (RJPZ 2) replaced its predecessor, the RJPZ 1, in 1967, using updated missile technology and boasting improved vehicle performance. The same SS-11 ATGW missile launchers were fitted, though the vehicle could carry 14 missiles as opposed to the 10 carried by the RJPZ 1. First produced in 1970, the TOW (Tube Launched, Optically tracked, Wire command link guided) anti-tank missile was developed by the American Hughes corporation and became the most widely used weapon of its kind in the world. The French-designed HOT (Haut-subsonique Optiquement Téléguidé Tiré d'un Tube) is a heavier missile with a range of between 250 and 13,200 ft (76 and 4023 m).

Front hull-mounted launchers

Two SS-11 launchers at the front of the hull created a 180-degree arc of traverse to the front of the vehicle. A 0.3 in (7.62 mm) MG3 machine gun was mounted on the top right-hand side of the hull, and another in the bow. The hull itself was the same as that used for the Jadgpanzer Kanone 4-5 self-propelled anti-tank gun.

The Raketenjagdpanzer represented a significant advance in anti-armor technology when it appeared in the 1960s, during one of the most dangerous phases of the Cold War.

Scorpion

Although the last Scorpion reconnaissance vehicles were withdrawn in 1994, some of their chassis remained in service as the Sabre, mounting a 1.18 in (30 mm) cannon turret taken from other AFVs.

A very light and compact AFV, the Scorpion could be airlifted to any part of the world by RAF Hercules transport aircraft.

COUNTRY OF ORIGIN: United Kingdom

CREW: 3

WEIGHT: 17,760 lb (8073 kg)

DIMENSIONS: length 15 ft 8.75 in (4.794 m); width 7 ft 4 in (2.235 m); height 2.102m (6ft 10.75in)

RANGE: 400 miles (644 km)

ARMOR: 0.5 in (12.7 mm)

ARMAMENT: one 2.99 in (76 mm) gun; one coaxial 0.30 in (7.62 mm) machine gun

POWERPLANT: one Jaguar 4.2-litre petrol engine developing 190 hp (142 kW)

PERFORMANCE: maximum road speed 50 mph (80 km/h); fording 3 ft 6 in (1.067 m); vertical obstacle 1 ft 8 in (0.50 m); trench 6 ft 9 in (2.057 m)

The first prototype of the Alvis Scorpion, officially named Combat Vehicle Reconnaissance (Tracked), appeared in 1969, following a British Army requirement for a tracked reconnaissance vehicle to replace the Saladin armored car.

Reconnaissance and high-speed advance

It entered service in 1972 and was exported to countries worldwide, particularly Belgium, where it was produced under license. The Scorpion was used in the battle for the Falkland Islands in 1982, crossing the marshy Falklands terrain with ease. During the final assault on Port Stanley, it acted in support of 2 Para. The Scorpion was used by the British Army, the Royal Air Force Regiment, and a dozen foreign customers. The Scorpion proved its value in both reconnaissance and in high-speed advances, but it has now been retired from British service. The Scorpion chassis has been used for a complete range of tracked vehicles, such as the Sultan, Spartan and Scimitar.

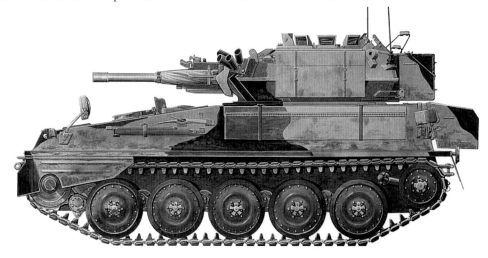

The original Scorpion was armed with a 2.99 in (76 mm) main gun, as seen here, but this was later replaced by a 1.18 in (30 mm) RARDEN cannon, as fitted to the Warrior infantry fighting vehicle.

T-72

The T-72 was the first Russian main battle tank to be the subject of an export drive to countries outside the Warsaw Pact area. One of its main attractions for customers was that it was relatively cheap.

COUNTRY OF ORIGIN: USSR

CREW: 3

WEIGHT: 85,568 lb (38,894 kg)

DIMENSIONS: length 30 ft 4 in (9.24 m); width 15 ft 7 in (4.75 m); height 7 ft 9 in (2.37 m)

RANGE: 434 miles (550 km)

ARMOR: classified

ARMAMENT: one 4.92 in (125 mm) gun; one 0.50 in (12.7 mm) anti-aircraft machine gun; one 0.30 in (7.62 mm) coaxial machine gun

POWERPLANT: one V-46 V-12 diesel engine developing 840 hp (626 kW)

PERFORMANCE: maximum road speed 50 mph (80 km/h); fording 4 ft 7 in (1.4 m); vertical obstacle 2 ft 9 in (0.85 m); trench 9 ft 2 in (2.8 m)

The T-72 tank operated by Iraq was no match for the coalition's armor.

The T-72 came into production in 1971. Smaller and faster than such tanks as the Chieftain, the T-72 was poorly armored with less versatility and effective firepower than its competitors. This became brutally clear in 1982 when Syrian T-72s proved no match for Israeli Merkava tanks and were knocked out in droves. The T-72 was designed for a conscript army and so is easy to operate and maintain, and is quite versatile. This accounts for its export success, being transferred to 14 other countries. It can be equipped for deep-fording, unlike most other tanks, within a matter of minutes, as well as being fully nuclear, biological and chemical (NBC) protected. Variants include a command vehicle, an anti-tank Cobra missile launcher and an armored recovery vehicle.

Used in fighting on both sides

The T-72 had the dubious distinction of fighting on both sides during the Gulf War of 1991, the Kuwaiti Army having taken delivery of the first of 200 tanks (the M-84 version) ordered from Yugoslavia. Iraq's Republican Guard is thought to have had about 1000 T-72s, which proved to be no match for the American M1 Abrams and the British Challenger.

The main armament is a 4.92 in (125 mm) smooth-bore gun with an automatic carousel loader, the charge above and the projectiles below. The weapon mounted on the commander's cupola is a 0.5 in (12.7 mm) anti-aircraft machine gun.

Type 74

The Type 74 main battle tank was fitted with hydro-pneumatic suspension, which enables the drive to adjust the height of the suspension to suit the type of terrain and also to improve the gun's elevation arc.

COUNTRY OF ORIGIN: Japan	
CREW: 3	
WEIGHT: 83,600 lb (38,000 kg)	
DIMENSIONS: length 28 ft 8 in (9.42 m); width 9 ft 10 in (3.2 m); height 7 ft 7 in (2.48 m)	
RANGE: 188 miles (300 km)	
ARMOR: classified	
ARMAMENT: one 4.13 in (105 mm) gun; one 0.30 in (7.62 mm) coaxial machine gun; one 0.50 in (12.7 mm) anti-aircraft machine gun; two smoke dischargers	
POWERPLANT: one 10ZF V-10 liquid-cooled diesel, developing 720 hp (536 kW)	
PERFORMANCE: maximum road speed: 34.4 mph (55 km/h); fording; 3 ft 4 in (1 m); vertical obstacle 3 ft 4 in (1 m); trench 8 ft 10 in (2.7 m)	

An unusual feature of the Type 74 is its hydro-pneumatic suspension, allowing the driver to adjust the height to suit the type of terrain.

The Type 74 main battle tank entered production on a small scale in late 1975, at a rate never rising above around 50 vehicles a year, which meant a very high unit cost. The tank has a laser rangefinder; computerized fire-control; and nuclear, biological and chemical (NBC) defense system as standard. However, the Type 74 has an unusual cross-linked hydro-pneumatic suspension system. This allows it to raise or lower different parts of the chassis in order to cross difficult terrain or to engage targets outside of the gun's normal elevation/depression range. Its turret was similar in design to that of the French AMX–30, with an automatic loader for the British L7A1 gun, which was later built under license by the Japan Steel Works. The JGSDF received 870 examples of the Type 74.

Ballistic computer and laser rangefinder

The fire control system includes a ballistic computer and laser rangefinder. Two specialized variants are the Type 78 armored recovery vehicle and the Type 87 mobile anti-aircraft vehicle. The Type 74 forms the basis of the Type 87 1.38 in (35 mm) self-propelled anti-aircraft gun tank.

The Type 74 has a well-sloped glacis plate with the driver's hatch on the upper left side, the turret being slightly forward of the hull center, with the engine compartment at the rear. The hull sides slope inwards and there are exhaust pipes in either side at the rear.

TAMSE TAM

The TAM medium tank was the Argentine Army's first modern armored fighting vehicle in this class, and went on to see limited operational use in counter-insurgency operations.

COUNTRY OF ORIGIN: Argentina

CREW: 4

WEIGHT: 67,100 lb (30,500 kg)

DIMENSIONS: length, gun forward 25 ft 2 in (8.23 m); width 9 ft 6 in (3.12 m); height 7 ft 5 in (2.42 m)

RANGE: 560 miles (900 km)

ARMOR: classified

ARMAMENT: one 4.13 in (105 mm) gun; one coaxial 0.30 in (7.62 mm) machine gun; one 0.30 in (7.62 mm) anti-aircraft machine gun

POWERPLANT: one V-6 turbo-charged diesel engine developing 720 hp (537 kW)

PERFORMANCE: maximum road speed: 46.9 mph (75 km/h); fording 4 ft 11 in (1.5 m); vertical obstacle 3 ft 3 in (1 m); trench 8 ft 2 in (2.5 m)

The TAM medium tank chassis was to have produced a whole family of fighting vehicles, but none has been placed in full production.

For years the Argentinian Army relied on World War II Sherman tanks for its armored forces. By the 1970s, these were becoming difficult to maintain. Most foreign tanks of the period were too heavy for domestic conditions and a new tank was ordered from Thyssen Henschel of West Germany. Once developed, production moved to Buenos Aires and production began towards the end of the 1970s.

Rocket launchers

The hull of the TAM was based on that of the MICV used by the West German Army. The armor is comparatively poor against that of other main battle tanks but is well sloped to give maximum protection. The tank was not built in time to have any impact on the 1982 Falklands conflict. Variants of the TAM were the VCA 155, comprising a lengthened TAM chassis fitted with the turret of an Italian Palmaria 6.10 in (155 mm) self-propelled howitzer, and the VCRT, an armored recovery vehicle that was built in prototype form only. Some TAMs were converted into rocket launchers.

Developed by Thyssen Henschel for the Argentine Army, the TAM was based on the well proven Marder chassis. The tank can have its operational range extended by fitting auxiliary fuel tanks at the rear of the hull.

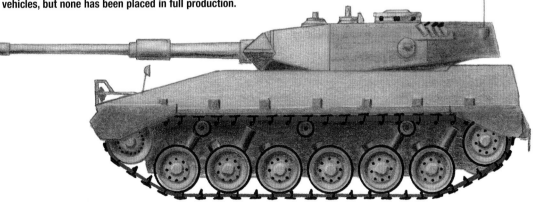

Leopard 2

The Leopard 2 is an extremely potent main battle tank and is one of the finest of its generation, offering a unique blend of firepower, protection and mobility. First delivered in 1978, it has been radically upgraded.

COUNTRY OF ORIGIN: West Germany

CREW: 4

WEIGHT: 120,960 lb (54,981 kg)

DIMENSIONS: length (with gun forward) 31 ft 8.7 in (9.668 m); length (hull) 25 ft 6 in (7.772 m); width 12 ft 1.7 in (3.7 m); height (overall) 9 ft 1.75 in (2.79 m)

RANGE: 342 miles (550 km)

ARMOR: classified

ARMAMENT: one 4.72 in (120 mm) gun; one coaxial 0.30 in (7.62 mm) machine gun; one 0.30 in (7.62 mm) anti–aircraft machine gun; eight smoke dischargers

POWERPLANT: one MTU 12-cylinder multi-fuel, developing 1,500 hp (1119 kW)

PERFORMANCE: maximum road speed 45 mph (72 km/h); fording 3 ft 3 in (1 m); vertical obstacle 3 ft 7.25 in (1.1 m); trench 9 ft 10 in (3 m)

The Leopard 2 A6EX, seen here, has the improved armor of the Bundeswehr's A5, allied to a longer 55-caliber gun.

The Leopard 2 was an offshoot of a cancelled joint development between the USA and West Germany in the late 1960s, the project being the MBT-70. But the West Germans continued the project and first production vehicles were delivered in 1977. Exports were soon equipping the Dutch Army. The Leopard 2 has a laser-rangefinder; thermal-imaging; a nuclear, biological and chemical (NBC) defense system; and amphibious capability. Its fire-system has combustible cartridge cases, so when the shell is fired, all that remains is the base of the cartridge, which frees up space. It has a 30 percent better power-to-weight ratio than the Leopard 1, which results in increased cross-country mobility and thus survivability.

Serving a range of nations

The latest Leopard variant is the 2A6. The Leopard 2 is in service with the armies of Austria, Denmark, Germany, the Netherlands, Norway, Switzerland, Sweden and Spain, with over 3,200 produced. The Finnish Army is buying 124 and the Polish Army acquired 128 surplus Leopard 2A4 tanks from Germany. In August 2005, Greece placed an order for 183 surplus Leopard 2A4 and 150 Leopard 1A5 tanks from German Army reserves.

Germany's excellent Leopard 2 tank has been a huge success story, and is in service with several NATO armies, as well as those of Sweden and Switzerland. The tank's capability is constantly being upgraded.

Khalid

When the Islamic revolution swept through Iran in 1979, many arms orders placed with western governments were abruptly cancelled. One of them was a tank called the Shir, which was then sold to Jordan as the Khalid.

COUNTRY OF ORIGIN: United Kingdom/Iran	
CREW: 4	
WEIGHT: 57 tons (58,000 kg)	
DIMENSIONS: length 21 ft 10 in (6.39 m); width 11 ft 7 in (3.42 m); height 9 ft 11 in (2/435 m)	
RANGE: 249 miles (400 km) (estimated)	
ARMOR: not available	
ARMAMENT: one 4.72 in (120 mm) L11A5 gun; two 0.30 in (7.62 mm) MGs	
POWERPLANT: Perkins Engines (Shrewsbury) Condor V-12 1200 12-cylinder diesel, water-cooled, developing 1200 hp (894.8 kW) at 2300 rpm	
PERFORMANCE: maximum speed: 43 mph (70 km/h)	

The Khalid was a very effective fighting vehicle and led to the UK government ordering its own version, the Challenger I.

In 1974, the Royal Ordnance factory at Leeds, Yorkshire, received a contract from the Iranian government for the production of 125 Shir 1 and 1225 Shir 2 main battle tanks. The Islamic revolution, with the overthrow of the Iranian royal dynasty and its government, upset this plan completely and the order was abruptly cancelled. Production of the Shir 1 had already started, and some rapid maneuvering by the British government secured an order from Jordan for 274 slightly modified Shir 1s under the name Khalid, these being delivered beginning in 1981. The tank was a late-production Chieftain with changes to the fire control system and powerpack. In fact, the Khalid represented such an important advance over the Chieftain that the British government ordered further development of the type, and it later emerged as the Challenger 1.

Name meaning sword

The name Khalid means sword in Arabic, and has since been applied to a much later main battle tank developed jointly by China and Pakistan. The Royal Ordnance factory was taken over by Vickers Defense Systems in 1986.

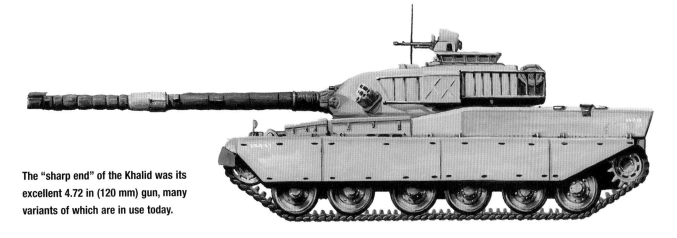

The "sharp end" of the Khalid was its excellent 4.72 in (120 mm) gun, many variants of which are in use today.

Olifant Mk IA

By far the best indigenous tank in service anywhere on the African continent, the Olifant owes it existence to the excellent Centurion, whose design has been refined and developed over half a century.

COUNTRY OF ORIGIN: South Africa

CREW: 4

WEIGHT: 123,200 lb (56,000 kg)

DIMENSIONS: length 30 ft (9.83 m); width 10 ft 4 in (3.38 m); height 8 ft 11 in (2.94 m)

RANGE: 313 miles (500 km)

ARMOR: 0.66–4.6 in (17–118 mm)

ARMAMENT: one 4.13 in (105 mm) gun; one 0.30 in (7.62 mm) coaxial machine gun; one 0.30 in (7.62 mm) anti-aircraft machine gun; two x 4 smoke dischargers

POWERPLANT: one V-12 air-cooled turbocharged diesel, developing 750 hp (559 kW)

PERFORMANCE: maximum road speed 28.1 mph (45 km/h); fording 4 ft 9 in (1.45 m); vertical obstacle 2 ft 11 in (0.9 m); trench 11 ft (3.352 m)

The Olifant Mk 1A is pictured with side armor panels removed to reveal the original bogie-type suspension.

Like the Israelis with their Sho't program, the South Africans took a basic Centurion tank and upgraded it to produce an indigenous main battle tank customized to their needs, with improved firepower and mobility. The fire control system of the Olifant ("Elephant") remained that of the original Centurion, but the tank was fitted with a hand-held laser rangefinder for the commander and image-intensifier for the gunner. The Olifant Mk 1A entered production in 1983, this variant having the same automotive system as the original Mk 1. The main armament change was the replacement of the 20-pounder gun with a locally built copy of the British 4.13 in (105 mm) L7 weapon (the new gun did retain the original breech mechanism).

Enhanced fire control systems

The Mk 1B version of the Olifant is much different, with a lengthened hull, new engine and transmission, and updated armor, as well as enhanced fire control systems. Variants include an armored recovery vehicle and repair vehicle. The Olifant is undoubtedly the best indigenous tank design on the African continent.

Traces of the original Centurion's design may still be seen in the hull of the Oliphant, but these vanished altogether when the tank underwent a complete rebuild to become the Oliphant Mk 2.

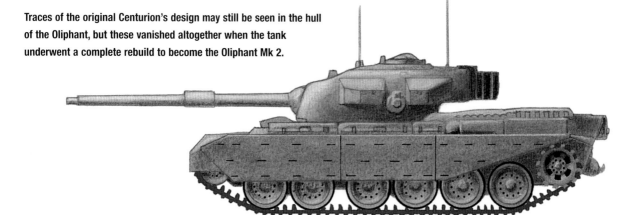

M1 Abrams

Capable of taking on the latest Russian-designed equipment and destroying it with almost ridiculous ease, America's M1 Abrams will certainly rank as one of the most effective tanks ever built.

COUNTRY OF ORIGIN: United States

CREW: 4

WEIGHT: 119,392 lb (54,269 kg)

DIMENSIONS: length 32 ft 0.5 in (9.766 m); width 12 ft (3.655 m); height 9 ft 6 in (2.895 m)

RANGE: 280 miles (450 km)

ARMOR: classified

ARMAMENT: one 4.13 in (105 mm) gun; two 0.30 in (7.62 mm) machine guns (one coaxial, one on loader's hatch); one 0.50 in (12.7 mm) machine gun

POWERPLANT: Avco Lycoming AGT-1500 gas turbine, developing 1,500 hp (1119 kW)

PERFORMANCE: maximum road speed 45 mph (72.5 km/h); fording 4 ft (1.219 m); vertical obstacle 4 ft 1 in (1.244 m); trench 9 ft (2.743 m)

All Abrams since the M1A1 have been equipped with the Rheinmetall 4.72 in (120 mm) smooth-bore gun, one of the most powerful of its kind in the world.

The M1 Abrams was the next stage in US tank development after the M60. Chrysler built the prototypes in 1978 and the first production vehicles appeared in 1980 with 30 tanks a month being built in following years.

The best protection

Its advanced Chobham armor makes the M1 the best-protected US main battle tank yet. Its gas turbine engine

is smaller and easier to service than a diesel engine, but the extra fuel requirement negates the space saved, which may be why the idea was rejected for the Leopard 2. Thermal sights, laser rangefinder and gun stabilization system give the M1 excellent firepower on the move, day or night. In the 1991 Gulf War, the Abrams knocked out Iraqi T-72s with impunity – no Abrams were destroyed by enemy fire. In the 2003 Iraq war, only a handful were lost. Production of M1A1 tanks for the US Army is complete. Over 8,800 M1 and M1A1 tanks have been produced for the US Army and Marine Corps, and the armies of Egypt, Saudi Arabia and Kuwait. The M1A1 is currently undergoing modernization, features of which include increased armor protection; suspension improvements; and a nuclear, biological and chemical (NBC) protection system that increases survivability in a contaminated environment.

The M1 Abrams main battle tank will always be remembered for its epic dash through the Iraqi desert during the Gulf War of 1991, the aim of the armored divisions using it being to cut off and destroy the elite Republican Guard.

T-80

Russia's T-80 main battle tank saw action in Chechnya, where it proved vulnerable to rocket-propelled grenades. As a result, the latest model incorporates very sophisticated defenses.

COUNTRY OF ORIGIN: USSR

CREW: 3

WEIGHT: 106,400 lb (48,363 kg)

DIMENSIONS: length 32 ft 6 in (9.9 m); width 11 ft 2 in (3.4 m); height 7 ft 3 in (2.2 m)

RANGE: 281 miles (450 km)

ARMOR: classified

ARMAMENT: one 4.92 in (125 mm) gun; one coaxial 0.30 in (7.62 mm) machine gun; one 0.50 in (12.7 mm) anti-aircraft machine gun

POWERPLANT: one multi-fuel gas turbine, developing 1000 hp (745 kW)

PERFORMANCE: maximum road speed 43.75 mph (70 km/h); fording 16 ft 5 in (5 m); vertical obstacle 3 ft 4 in (1 m); trench 9 ft 4 in (2.85 m)

The T-80UK, seen here, is a command tank variant and is fitted with a Shtora-1 defensive system.

The T-80 entered service with the Soviet Red Army in the mid-1980s. Like the T-72 tank, it had an automatic loader for the main gun, allowing the crew to be kept to a minimum of three.

High manufacturing costs

The main gun was a standard fully stabilized 4.92 in (125 mm) weapon as fitted in the T-72, but could fire a much greater range of ammunition, including depleted uranium rounds for extra armor-piercing capability. A laser rangefinder led to an improved fire-control system.

Like all Soviet tanks, the T-80 could make its own smoke screen and had four dischargers on the hull for launching chaff or decoys to distract enemy missiles. Adjustable ground clearance provided extra cross-country mobility. Despite ongoing problems with the engine and manufacturing costs, which were much higher in the event than had been anticipated, the T-80 underwent several upgrades, the first of which produced the T-80B in 1982. This was followed, in the mid-1980s, by the T-80U, which was equipped to fire the NK112 AT-8 Songster laser-beam-riding missile. The latest version, the T-80UM-1 Bars (Snow Leopard) is fitted with very advanced anti-missile equipment.

Developed from the T-72, the Russian T-80 main battle tank first entered service in 1976 and was the first production tank in the world to be fitted with a gas turbine engine.

Type 69

China exported thousands of her Type 69 variant of the Russian T-55. Many of these were delivered to Iran and Iraq, and fought one another during the long "oil war" between those two countries in the 1980s.

COUNTRY OF ORIGIN: China	
CREW: 4	
WEIGHT: 80,300 lb (36,500 kg)	
DIMENSIONS: length 26 ft 6 in (8.68 m); width 10 ft 1 in (3.3 m); height 8 ft 10 in (2.87 m)	
RANGE: 250 miles (375 km)	
ARMOR: 3.94 in (100 mm)	
ARMAMENT: one 3.94 in (100 mm) gun; one 0.50 in (12.7 mm) machine gun; two 0.30 in (7.62 mm) machine guns; two smoke rocket dischargers	
POWERPLANT: one V-12 liquid-cooled diesel engine developing 580 hp (432 kW)	
PERFORMANCE: maximum road speed: 31.3 mph (50 km/h); fording 4 ft 7 in (1.4 m); vertical obstacle 2 ft 7 in (0.8 m); trench 8 ft 10 in (2.7 m)	

A regiment of Type 69 tanks parades at a military review outside Beijing. The Type 69 is an improved and upgraded version of the T-59.

The Type 69 replaced the Type 59. First seen in public in 1982 during a parade in Beijing, the tank still resembled the Type 59, but was fitted with a new 4.13–4.17 in (105–106 mm) gun, likely based on that of the Soviet T-62, examples of which were captured by the Chinese during border clashes with the USSR. There are a number of variants, including a self-propelled anti-aircraft gun, armored bridge-layer and armored recovery vehicle. The latter has a Type 69 chassis with the turret removed and replaced by a superstructure; there is a dozer blade at the front and crane at the rear. The Type 69 was only fully accepted for service with the PLA in 1982, and then only in limited quantities, as the Chinese Army was still not satisfied with its performance.

A successful export

When the tank was offered for export it was an immediate success, over 2000 being sold in the 1980s. Large numbers were sold to Iraq in the early 1980s, with Saudi Arabia acting as intermediary, to make up for losses experienced during the war with Iran.

The tank pictured here is a Type 69II, armed with a 4.13 in (105 mm) main gun and a heavy machine gun. The Type 69 was still in production up to the late 1990s, and about 6000 are estimated to have been built.

Merkava

First used in action during Israel's invasion of Lebanon in 1982, the Merkava main battle tank was developed to avoid the nation's dependence on imports of armored fighting vehicles.

COUNTRY OF ORIGIN: Israel

CREW: 4

WEIGHT: 122,976 lb (55,898 kg)

DIMENSIONS: length 27 ft 5.25 in (8.36 m); width 12 ft 2.5 in (3.72 m); height 8 ft 8 in (2.64 m)

RANGE: 310 miles (500 km)

ARMOR: classified

ARMAMENT: one 4.13 in (105 mm) rifled gun; one 0.30 in (7.62 mm) machine gun

POWERPLANT: one Teledyne Continental AVDS-1790-6A V-12 diesel engine developing 900 hp (671 kW)

PERFORMANCE: maximum road speed 28.6 mph (46 km/h); vertical obstacle 3 ft 3.3 in (1 m); trench 9 ft 10 in (3 m)

Prior to the Six Day War in 1967, Israel had relied on Sherman and Centurion tanks. Doubts as to future supplies and also concerns that these tanks did not fully meet Israeli requirements prompted development of an indigenous tank. The first Merkavas appeared in 1980 and saw action against Syrian forces in Lebanon in 1982.

Crew survival and rough terrain

Compared to other modern main battle tanks, the Merkava is slow and has a poor power-to-weight ratio, but it is designed for specific tactical requirements. The emphasis is on crew survivability, which explains the Merkava's small cross-section, which makes it less of a target, and well sloped armor for greatest protection. The tank is optimized for operations in the rough terrain of northern Israel and the Golan Heights and is unusual in layout, with the engine at the front and the fighting compartment to the rear. This gives enhanced frontal protection while the ammunition, kept at the back, is not only in the safest place but is also quite easily stowed in the vehicle through a rear door, making replenishment in the combat zone much safer.

The Merkava was first used in combat in the 1982 invasion of Lebanon in 1982, where it engaged and defeated Syrian T-72s.

The Merkava is equipped with an identification friend/foe system, mounted on either side of the turret, for the identification of friendly fighting vehicles. It also has a threat warning system.

Type 80

China's Type 80 main battle tank is fundamentally a Type 69 with a redesigned hull and improvements in armor and fire control system.

The Type 80 is well equipped for battlefield mobility, carrying jettison-able fuel tanks, an unditching beam and a snorkel tube.

COUNTRY OF ORIGIN: China	
CREW: 4	
WEIGHT: 83,600 lb (38,000 kg)	
DIMENSIONS: length 28 ft 6 in (9.33 m); width 10 ft 4 in (3.37 m); height 7 ft (2.3 m)	
RANGE: 356 miles (570 km)	
ARMOR: classified	
ARMAMENT: one 4.13 in (105 mm) gun; one 0.30 in (7.62 mm) coaxial machine gun; one 0.50 in (12.7 mm) coaxial machine gun	
POWERPLANT: one V-12 diesel engine developing 730 hp (544 kW); manual transmission	
PERFORMANCE: maximum road speed: 37.5 mph (60 km/h); fording 4 ft 7 in (1.4 m); vertical obstacle 2 ft 7 in (0.8 m); trench 8 ft 10 in (2.7 m)	

The Chinese Type 80 main battle tank was a development of the T-69 series but with a brand new hull, a larger main armament and a more modern computerized fire-control system, which includes a laser rangefinder, mounted either over the gunner's sights, or over the 4.13 in (105 mm) gun itself.

Easily uparmored

The vehicle carries a snorkel that can be fitted to allow for deep fording. It has an in-built fire-detection/ suppression system and can be easily uparmored (with composite armor plates) to give increased battlefield survivability. Crew configuration is as follows: the driver sits at the front left with some of the ammunition, while the loader, commander and gunner sit in the turret. Five hundred

units were built for the Chinese People's Liberation Army, and a few, not exceeding 20, were supplied to Myanmar (Burma). Another standard item of equipment is a ditching beam, and extra range can be achieved with the aid of two auxiliary fuel tanks at the rear of the vehicle, which can be jettisoned when empty.

The battlefield survivability of China's Type 80 main battle tank has been much enhanced by the addition of composite armor, but it cannot be described as a sophisticated fighting vehicle, though it packs a considerable punch.

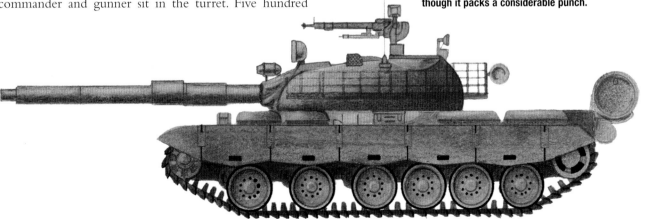

AMX-40

Although it represented a significant improvement over its predecessor, the AMX-30, the AMX-40 was intended solely for export, which meant that the French Army had to wait for the advent of the very advanced Leclerc.

COUNTRY OF ORIGIN: France

CREW: 4

WEIGHT: 94,600 lb (43,000 kg)

DIMENSIONS: length 32 ft 11.3 in (10.04 m); width 11 ft 0.3 in (3.36 m); height 10 ft 1.3 in (3.08 m)

RANGE: 373 miles (600 km)

ARMOR: classified

ARMAMENT: one 4.72 in (120 mm) gun; one 0.78 in (20 mm) cannon in cupola; one 0.30 in (7.62 mm) machine gun

POWERPLANT: one Poyaud 12-cylinder diesel engine developing 1100 hp (820 kW)

PERFORMANCE: maximum road speed 44 mph (70 km/h); fording 4 ft 3 in (1.30 m); vertical obstacle 3 ft 2.4 in (1 m); trench 10 ft 6 in (3.20 m)

It was a viable fighting vehicle but, unluckily, France's AMX-40 was produced at the wrong time to capture its intended export markets.

Unlike the Americans, British and Germans, the French did not develop a second generation of heavy main battle tanks comparable to the M1A1 Abrams, Challenger or Leopard 2, so there was a hefty delay before the Leclerc could be deployed.

An improvement on its predecessor

Designed in the early 1980s, primarily for export, the GIAT-built AMX-40 was a significant improvement on its predecessor, the AMX-30, in the key areas of armor, mobility and firepower. The tank has a laser rangefinder, gun stabilization equipment and a low-light

television for night-fighting. One interesting feature is the ammunition stowage. Carried in the turret and surrounded by bulkheads, the ammunition compartment is designed so that if it is hit, the ammunition will explode upwards, away from the crew below. As it was intended for export, the French Army was forced to rely on the AMX-30 until the advent of the Leclerc. The AMX-40 carries four crew, the traditional number for a main battle tank: (commander, gunner, radio operator and driver).

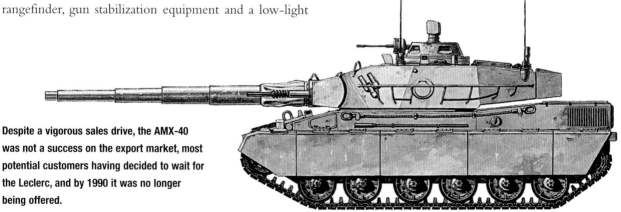

Despite a vigorous sales drive, the AMX-40 was not a success on the export market, most potential customers having decided to wait for the Leclerc, and by 1990 it was no longer being offered.

Challenger 1

The Challenger 1 main battle tank was a development of the Shir 2 tank ordered by Iran, but cancelled following the Islamic revolution. Challenger 1 suffered from an inadequate fire control system.

COUNTRY OF ORIGIN: United Kingdom

CREW: 4

WEIGHT: 136,400 lb (62,000 kg)

DIMENSIONS: length, gun forward: 35 ft 4 in (11.56 m); width 10 ft 8 in (3.52 m); height 7 ft 5 in (2.5 m)

RANGE: 250 miles (400 km)

ARMOR: classified

ARMAMENT: one 4.72 in (120 mm) gun; two 0.30 in (7.62 mm) machine guns; two smoke dischargers

POWERPLANT: one liquid-cooled diesel engine developing 1200 hp (895 kW)

PERFORMANCE: maximum road speed: 35 mph (55 km/h); fording 3 ft 4 in (1 m); vertical obstacle 2 ft 10 in (0.9 m); trench 9 ft 2 in (2.8 m)

A Challenger 1 on maneuvers in Germany. The tank was withdrawn from British Army service in 2000.

The Challenger 1 was introduced in 1982 to replace the Chieftain. It reflected British thinking on tank design, being heavily armed and armored. It was slower than contemporary Warsaw Pact vehicles, but made up for it with its composite Chobham armor, which was virtually impenetrable to enemy rounds, and the greater accuracy of its armament. In any case, NATO thinking regarding the war in central Europe with the forces of the Soviet Union and her allies always placed the emphasis on defense and holding enemy forces until reinforcements arrived. Its armor and nimbleness, despite its lack of speed, allow for good survivability. In 1990, 180 Challengers were deployed to Saudi Arabia from Germany, and these put up a creditable performance during Operation Desert Storm early in the following year, destroying 300 enemy AFVs with no loss to themselves.

Slow rate of fire

Its main drawback was a poor fire control and sighting system, which resulted in a slow rate of fire. This defect was remedied in a revised version, the Challenger 2. The Challenger 1 is no longer in UK service.

The Challenger 1 was similar to late-production versions of the Chieftain in most respects, and with its powerful L11A5 rifled gun, it gave the British Army's armored formations a potent weapon.

ENGESA EE-T1 Osorio

Like Sweden, Brazil has taken pains to dispense with reliance on the major powers for the supply of military equipment. One indigenous design was the EE-T1 main battle tank.

The Osorio was a bold attempt by Brazil to break into the main battle tank market, but its capability fell far short of competitors.

COUNTRY OF ORIGIN: Brazil

CREW: 4

WEIGHT: 85,800 lb (39,000 kg)

DIMENSIONS: length 32 ft 9.5 in (9.995 m); width 10 ft 8.3 in (3.26 m); height 7 ft 9.3 in (2.371 m)

RANGE: 342 miles (550 km)

ARMOR: classified

ARMAMENT: one British 4.13 in (105 mm)/French 4.72 in (120 mm) gun; one 0.30 in (7.62 mm) machine gun

POWERPLANT: one 12-cylinder diesel engine developing 1000 hp (745 kW)

PERFORMANCE: maximum road speed 43.5 mph (70 km/h); fording 3 ft 11 in (1.20 m); vertical obstacle 3 ft 4 in (1.15 m); trench 9 ft 10 in (3.0 m)

Designed to meet both home and export markets, the first prototype Osorio was completed in 1985. The layout is conventional with laser rangefinder, stabilizers to allow firing while on the move and thermal-imaging cameras, as well as a full nuclear, biological and chemical (NBC) defense system.

Two sizes of main gun

The tank can be fitted with two different sizes of main gun. Variants include a bridge-layer, armored recovery vehicle and an anti-aircraft gun vehicle. There is little innovation in the design of the Osorio compared to the latest designs being produced in Europe and the United States. Nonetheless, it is attractive for countries with no capacity to build their own main battle tank, and for whom the European and US tanks are too costly and complex. Despite the Osario's attractions, the Engesa company was unable to secure any sales for it. A promised Saudi government order in 1989 for 318 Osarios fell through, and no contract was signed. In addition, the 1991 Gulf War proved that the Osario could not compete with the American Abrams or Britain's Challenger.

If the Osario had been adopted by the Royal Saudi Army, it would have been named Al Fahd, which means Lion of the Desert.

Type 88

The Type 88 K1, a smaller version of the M1 Abrams main battle tank, was developed to meet the threat posed by North Korea's Russian-built T-62s. It has a fully computerized fire control system.

COUNTRY OF ORIGIN: South Korea

CREW: 4

WEIGHT: 114,400 lb (52,000 kg)

DIMENSIONS: length 29 ft 6 in (9.67 m); width 10 ft 11 in (3.59 m); height: 6 ft 10 in (2.25 m)

RANGE: 313 miles (500 km)

ARMOR: classified

ARMAMENT: one 4.13 in (105 mm) gun; one 0.30 in (7.62 mm) coaxial machine gun; one 0.50 in (12.7 mm) anti-aircraft machine gun; 2 x 6 smoke dischargers

POWERPLANT: one liquid-cooled turbocharged diesel, developing 1200 hp (895 kW)

PERFORMANCE: maximum road speed 40.6 mph (65 km/h); fording 3 ft 11 in (1.2 m); vertical obstacle 3 ft 4 in (1 m)

South Korea is balanced on a knife edge, with North Korea as an unstable neighbor. The Type 88 is a vital weapon in her armory.

Also known as the K1, the Type 88 was developed by General Dynamics in the early 1980s in response to a South Korean requirement for a main battle tank to be built locally. Series production was undertaken by the Hyundai Precision and Industrial Company at Changwon in 1985/86. Possession of the K1 gave the Republic of Korea Army the means to outfit the North Koreans' T-62s, seen as a main threat for some time.

Environmental sensor package

The main smooth-bore armament has a thermal sleeve and fume extractor and uses a computerized fire-control system based on the M1 ballistic computer and an environmental sensor package. The vehicle has a nuclear, biological and chemical (NBC) system designed to give individual crew protection. Its successor, the K1A1, is now in service, armed with a larger 4.72 in (120 mm) smooth-bore gun and improved fire control system. An AVLB variant, based on the K1 chassis, has been designed in the UK and 56 were ordered by the South Koreans. The tank has not been exported. The variant developed for this purpose was designated K1M.

The Type 88 K1A1 includes an improved fire-control system featuring thermal image KGPS (Korean Gunner's Primary Sight), KCPS (Korean Commander's Panoramic Sight) and a new 32-bit ballistic computer.

Stingray Light Tank

Although the Stingray light tank carries only light armor, it is a competent fighting vehicle that combines good firepower with excellent mobility, and is intended for the export market.

COUNTRY OF ORIGIN: United States

CREW: 5

WEIGHT: 69,000 lb (31,360 kg)

DIMENSIONS: length 19 ft 4 in (5.9 m); width 8 ft 7 in (2.6 m); height 9 ft (2.74 m)

RANGE: 100 miles (161 km)

ARMOR: 0.59–2.99 in (15–76 mm)

ARMAMENT: one 2.95 in (75 mm) gun; one coaxial 0.30 in (7.62 mm) machine gun; 0.50 in (12.7 mm) anti-aircraft gun on turret

POWERPLANT: twin General Motors 6-71 diesel engines developing 500 hp (373 kW)

PERFORMANCE: maximum road speed 29 mph (46.4 km/h); fording 3 ft (0.9 m); vertical obstacle 2 ft (0.61 m); trench 7 ft 5 in (2.26 m)

The Stingray light tank was designed by Textron Marine and Land Systems (formerly Cadillac Gage Textron) as a private venture, the company having identified a requirement for a light and highly mobile AFV with the hitting power of a main battle tank. The first prototype was completed in 1985, and went to Thailand for operational trials and evaluation, after which the Thai Army placed an order for 106 examples.

Thai Stingrays

The firm went on to develop a more advanced version, the Stingray II, which appeared in 1996. It had a more capable digital fire control system and NBC equipment. The primary armament of the Stingray is the LRF (Low Recoil Force) version of the British L7 series 4.13 in (105 mm) rifled gun. Up to 2007, the only export order for Stingray has come from Thailand, which took delivery of 100 vehicles in 1988–90. Despite claims that the vehicle combines the lethal qualities of a main battle tank with high mobility, it is too lightly armored for any real battlefield role, and is in effect a reconnaissance tank. The Thai order was completed in 1990.

The sides of the pointed turret slope inwards, with a turret basket at the rear. Smoke grenade dischargers are carried on each side.

Stingray is the largest of the private-venture fighting vehicles developed by Cadillac Gage and is optimized for the reconnaissance role; it is not designed to engage heavy armor on the battlefield.

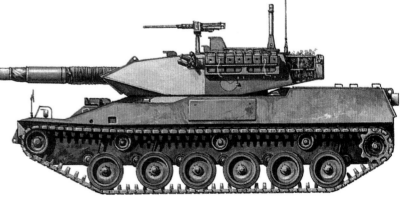

Type 85

The Type 85 series of main battle tanks has a mutual origin in the Russian T-54/55, but have undergone such a degree of development over the years that it is hard to recognize any common features.

COUNTRY OF ORIGIN: China

CREW: 3

WEIGHT: 90,200 lb (41,000 kg)

DIMENSIONS: length 31 ft 5 in (10.28 m); width: 10 ft 6 in (3.45 m); height: 7 ft (2.3 m)

RANGE: 312 miles (500 km)

ARMOR: classified

ARMAMENT: one 4.92 in (125 mm) gun; one 0.30 in (7.62 mm) coaxial machine gun; one 0.50 in (12.7 mm) anti-aircraft machine gun; two smoke grenade launchers

POWERPLANT: one V-12 supercharged diesel engine developing 730 hp (544 kW)

PERFORMANCE: maximum road speed 35.8 mph (57.25 km/h); fording 4 ft 7 in (1.4 m); vertical obstacle 2 ft 7 in (0.8 m); trench 8 ft 10 in (2.7 m)

Based on the mechanical features of the old T-54, the Type 85 incorporates so many changes that it is virtually a new design.

The Type 85 main battle tank entered production on a small scale in the late 1980s, based on the chassis of the Type 80.

Chinese innovation

In an innovation for Chinese tanks, it had an all-welded turret instead of the usual cast steel type, armor being increased all round. It also had better communications equipment. The increased main armament (4.92 in [125 mm], not the 4.13 in [105 mm] of the Type 80) is fed by an automatic loader, which allows the crew to be reduced to a minimum. However, space inside is reduced by the ammunition being made up of separate projectile and charge. The Type 85, still in production, has been exported to Pakistan, where it is known as the Type 85-IIM. The Type 85 was officially designated by the PLA as Type 96 and entered service with the PLA armored forces from 1997. The PLA had reportedly received over 1500 examples of the Type 96 by 2005. Recent photos released by Chinese state media confirmed that all of the PLA's elite armored divisions are now equipped with the Type 96 MBT. It is still inferior to American and European tanks.

The Type 85/96 is one of the Chinese People's Liberation Army's latest tanks, and shows many improvements over previous models. The tank is equipped with a Russian-type autoloader.

C1 Ariete

The Ariete main battle tank is one of a family of three armored vehicles, the others being the Centauro tank destroyer and the Dardo infantry fighting vehicle. The Italian Army has 200 in service.

COUNTRY OF ORIGIN: Italy

CREW: 4

WEIGHT: 118,800 lb (54,000 kg)

DIMENSIONS: length 29 ft 6 in (9.67 m); width 11 ft (3.6 m); height: 7 ft 7 in (2.5 m)

RANGE: 375 miles (600 km)

ARMOR: classified

ARMAMENT: one 4.72 in (120 mm) gun; one 0.30 in (7.62 mm) coaxial machine gun; one 0.30 in (7.62 mm) anti-aircraft machine gun; 2 x 4 smoke dischargers

POWERPLANT: one IVECO FIAT MTCA V-12 turbocharged diesel engine developing 1250 hp (932 kW)

PERFORMANCE: maximum road speed 41.3 mph (66 km/h); fording 3 ft 11 in (1.2 m); vertical obstacle 6 ft 11 in (2.1 m); trench 9 ft 10 in (3 m)

The Ariete incorporates an additional layer of advancd armor over the frontal arc, offering protection against modern HEAT warheads.

The C1 Ariete main battle tank was built in response to a 1982 specification of the Italian Army for a replacement for its obsolete M47 Pattons. With its special composite armor, it has the typical slab-sided look of modern main battle tanks. It was built by a consortium formed in 1984 by Otobreda and Iveco to develop a new family of armored fighting vehicles for the Italian Army. First deliveries of the Ariete were made in December 1995, the last examples being issued in 2002. The Ariete is of an all-steel welded construction, with composite armor on the hull front and turret front and sides, and side-skirts protecting the top of the tracks. It is conventional in layout, with the driver at the front right, a power-operated turret in the center, gunner on the right, loader on the left and the powerplant at the rear of the vehicle.

High single-shot probability

The main smooth-bore armament has a thermal sleeve and fume extractor and uses the latest Galileo computerized fire-control system, the thermal-vision night sight and laser rangefinder giving high single-shot kill probability, moving or stationary. An armored recovery vehicle and AVLB based on the C1 chassis are expected to follow.

A distinguishing feature of the Ariete is the installation of four smoke grenade launchers on either side of the turret. The grenades are automatically discharged when the tank's laser warning system detects a threat.

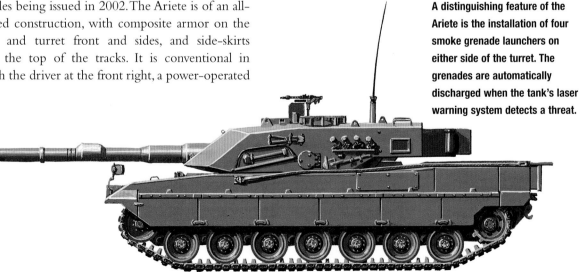

Leclerc

Named after the famous French general of World War II, whose 2nd Armored Division liberated Paris in 1944, the Leclerc is one of the finest main battle tanks in the world.

COUNTRY OF ORIGIN: France

CREW: 3

WEIGHT: 117,700 lb (53,500 kg)

DIMENSIONS: length 30 ft (9.87 m); width 11 ft 4 in (3.71 m); height 7 ft 6 in (2.46 m)

RANGE: 345 miles (550 km)

ARMOR: classified

ARMAMENT: one 4.72 in (120 mm) gun; one 0.50 in (12.7 mm) machine gun; one 0.30 in (7.62 mm) machine gun; 3 x 9 smoke dischargers

POWERPLANT: one SAEM UDU V8X 1500 T9 Hyperbar eight-cylinder diesel engine developing 1500 hp; SESM ESM500 automatic transmission

PERFORMANCE: maximum road speed 45.6 mph (73 km/h); fording 3 ft 3 in (1 m); vertical obstacle 4 ft 1 in (1.25 m); trench 9 ft 10 in (3 m)

A Leclerc main battle tank leads the Bastille Day parade down the Champs-Elysées in Paris. It is an excellent vehicle.

The Leclerc was designed to replace the French Army's fleet of AMX-30 tanks. Development began in 1983, and the first production Leclercs appeared in 1991. For many years the French Army had to rely on the ageing AMX-30 main battle tank as its principal armored spearhead; the Leclerc, with its powerful 4.72 in (120 mm) gun and advanced fire control electronics, has given France's armored divisions a new dimension. An automatic loading system for the main armament and remote-control machine guns allow the crew to be cut down to three. The tank can be fitted with extra fuel tanks to increase operational range, and standard equipment includes a fire-detection/suppression system, thermal-imaging and laser rangefinder for the main gun, and a land navigation system.

Integrated electronic systems

The onboard electronic systems are fully integrated to allow automatic reconfiguration in case of battlefield failure or damage. As well as those in French service, around 390 Leclercs have been exported to the United Arab Emirates.

The Leclerc main battle tank is a very effective fighting machine and incorporates all that is good in French tank design. It gives the French Army an armored capability that is second to none in the world today.

Type 90

The Type 90 main battle tank is widely considered to be one of the most advanced MBTs in the world. With over 200 in service with the Japanese Ground Defense Force, it forms a large part of Japan's armored power.

The Type 90 is considered one of the most advanced MBTs in its class, incorporating composite armor for the hull and turret.

COUNTRY OF ORIGIN: Japan

CREW: 3

WEIGHT: 110,000 lb (50,000 kg)

DIMENSIONS: length 29 ft 10 in (9.76 m); width 10 ft 5 in (3.4 m); height 7 ft 1 in (2.34 m)

RANGE: 219 miles (350 km)

ARMOR: classified

Armament: one 4.72 in (120 mm) gun; one 0.30 in (7.62 mm) coaxial machine gun; one 0.50 in (12.7 mm) anti-aircraft machine gun; two smoke dischargers

POWERPLANT: one 10ZG V-10 fuel-injection diesel, developing 1500 hp (1118 kW)

PERFORMANCE: maximum road speed 43.8 mph (70 km/h); fording 6 ft 6 in (2 m); vertical obstacle 3 ft 4 in (1 m); trench 8 ft 10 in (2.7m)

The Type 90 main battle tank was placed in development in the mid-1970s to meet the needs of the Japanese Ground Self-Defense Force. It entered production on a small scale in 1992. Its slow production rate makes this the most expensive unit cost tank produced by any nation in the world. The vehicle carries a laser rangefinder, computerized fire control and NBC system as standard, as well as thermal-imaging and night-driving capability. Like the Type 74, the vehicle has a cross-linked hydro-pneumatic suspension system, which allows it to raise or lower different parts of the chassis in order to cross difficult terrain or to engage targets outside of the gun's normal elevation/depression range.

Crew of three only

No loader is required, an automatic loading system being provided for the 4.72 in (120 mm) gun, which fires HEAT-MP and APFSDS-T rounds with a semi-combustible cartridge case. The gunner aims and fires the main armament, moving or stationary, with a high probability of a first-round hit. Variants include the Type 90 ARV with dozer blade and winch and the Type 91 AVLB bridge-layer.

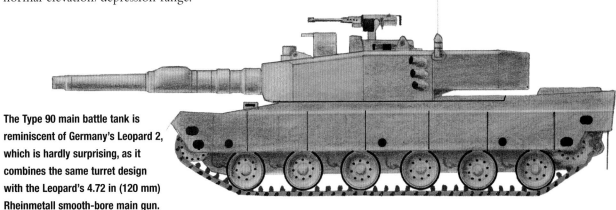

The Type 90 main battle tank is reminiscent of Germany's Leopard 2, which is hardly surprising, as it combines the same turret design with the Leopard's 4.72 in (120 mm) Rheinmetall smooth-bore main gun.

T-90

Russia's T-90 tank is the latest descendant of the T-72 line, and is in service in substantial numbers. It has also been purchased by India, which has made further modifications to it.

COUNTRY OF ORIGIN: Russia

CREW: 3

WEIGHT: 45.76 tons (46,500 kg)

DIMENSIONS: length (hull) 22 ft 6 in (6.86 m); width 11 ft 1 in (3.37 m); height 7 ft 4 in (2.23 m)

RANGE: 400 miles (650 km)

ARMOR: unknown

ARMAMENT: one 4.92 in (125 mm) 2A46M Rapira 3 smooth-bore gun; one co-axial 0.3 in (7.62 mm) PKT MG; one 0.5 in (12.7 mm) NSVT AA MG

POWERPLANT: V-84MS 12-cylinder multi-fuel diesel, 840 hp (627 kW) at 2000 rpm

PERFORMANCE: maximum road speed 40 mph (65 km/h); fording 3 ft 11 in (1.2 m); trench 9 ft (2.8 m); 2 ft 9 in (0.85 m)

The T-90 has been marketed as a new tank, but it is actually an upgrade of the T-72. The turret is fitted with Kontakt-5 reactive armor.

The T-90 main battle tank is the most modern in service with the Russian Army, and is a further development of the T-72. It entered production in 1993 and has some subsystems of the T-80. It also features the latest development of the Kontakt-5 explosive reactive armor, which provides protection against chemical and kinetic energy warheads. By the mid-1990s, more than 100 T-90s were in service with armored units in the Russian Far Eastern Military District. In 1996 an upgraded model made its appearance, featuring a fully welded turret in place of the original T-90's cast turret. In 2006 there were 241 T-90s serving with the Russian Army's 5th Tank Division in the Siberian Military District.

Build-your-own tank kit

In 2001, India, faced with a shortfall in modern armor following the debacle of its indigenous Arjun MBT design, purchased 310 T-90S tanks from Russia, 120 being delivered complete and the rest in kit form for local assembly. India has also developed an improved version of the T-90S, known as the Bhishma. The name means "He of the Terrible Oath."

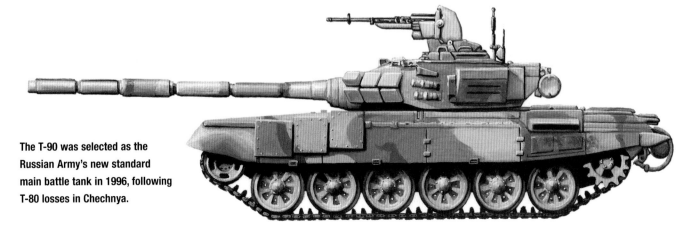

The T-90 was selected as the Russian Army's new standard main battle tank in 1996, following T-80 losses in Chechnya.

PT-91

By upgrading the Russian T-72, the Polish Army has fielded a viable main battle tank that will remain at the core of its armored divisions for some time and has avoided the need to purchase expensive new-build equipment.

COUNTRY OF ORIGIN: Poland

CREW: 3

WEIGHT: 44.6 tons (45,300 kg)

DIMENSIONS: length 22 ft 10 in (6.95 m); width 11 ft 9 in (3.59 m); height 7 ft 2 in (2.19 m)

RANGE: 405 miles (650 km)

ARMOR: unknown

ARMAMENT: One 4.92 in (125 mm) gun; one 0.3 in (7.62 mm) MG; one 0.5 in (12.7 mm) AA MG

POWERPLANT: S-12U V-12 supercharged diesel, 850 hp (634 kW) at 2300 rpm

PERFORMANCE: maximum road speed 38 mph (60 km/h); vertical obstacle 9 ft 2 in (2.8 m); trench 16 ft 5 in (5 m)

This PT-91 is seen with its hull and turret covered by explosive reactive armor (ERA) plates.

The Polish PT-91 main battle tank is a much-modified version of the Russian T-72M1, and is the outcome of a program, initiated by the Polish Ministry of Defense in the late 1980s, aimed at modernizing the later models of the Soviet tanks that were in Polish Army service. The Polish Army had already upgraded its T-55 tanks to T-55AM standard, and it was decided to implement a similar project with the T-72M1. Work was slow at first, as the Polish General Staff was considering the purchase of a new T-72 variant, the T-72S, but this came to nothing when the Soviet Union fragmented and as a result work on the upgraded T-72M1 was accelerated. The modernized tank, designated PT-91 Twardy (the name means "hardy") entered service in 1995.

Modernized and redesignated PT–91A

Changes from the T-72 include a new dual-axis stabilized fire-control system, reactive armor, a more powerful 850-hp S12-U engine, and hydraulic transmission with seven foward gears and one reverse. In 1995 the PT-91 Twardy was given a 1000-hp engine, a more advanced fire-control system and automatic loader and was designated PT-91A.

Following an international competition, Malaysia selected the enhanced PT-91 to meet its future main battle tank requirements.

Arjun

The Indian Army made a bold attempt to produce its own indigenous main battle tank with the Arjun, eliminating the need to buy foreign material, but its plans went wrong.

COUNTRY OF ORIGIN: India

CREW: 4

WEIGHT: 127,600 lb (58,000 kg)

DIMENSIONS: length 32 ft 2 in (9. 8m); width 10 ft 5 in (3.17 m); height 8 ft (2.44 m)

RANGE: 250 miles (400 km)

ARMOR: classified

ARMAMENT: one 4.72 in (120 mm) gun; one 0.30 in (7.62 mm) machine gun

POWERPLANT: one MTU MB 838 Ka 501 water-cooled diesel developing 1400 hp (1044 kW)

PERFORMANCE: maximum road speed 45 mph (72 km/h); fording 3 ft 3 in (1 m); vertical gradient 3 ft 7 in (1.1 m); trench 9 ft 10 in (3 m)

The Indian Army's long experience with tanks of Soviet design is reflected in the configuration of the Arjun.

The Arjun is India's first indigenous main battle tank design. The Indian Army's Combat Vehicle Research and Development Establishment had many problems with the project, resulting in delays that held up the in-service date. Thereafter, the Arjun program was constantly beset by delays and cost escalations, and it was not until 2004 that the first 15 tanks (out of an order for 124) were activated by the Indian Army. Some senior Indian Army officers saw the Arjun as a "white elephant" and advocated purchasing more T-90s from Russia as a much more viable alternative. One of the main problems was the lack of an indigenous powerplant, forcing India to use a German MTU diesel.

Locally designed armament

The Arjun's main armament is a locally designed stabilized 4.72 in (120 mm) rifled gun able to fire ammunition types such as high explosive, high explosive anti-tank and high explosive squash head. The tank has an advanced fire-control system integrated with a combined day/night thermal-imaging gunner's assembly with built-in laser rangefinder. In addition, there is a full weather-sensor package.

India's attempt to produce its own indigenous main battle tank was frustrated by continual delays and setbacks, and was seen by many senior army officers as a retrograde step.

Challenger 2

The design of the Challenger 2 main battle tank incorporates many of the lessons learned during combat operations by its predecessor, Challenger 1, in the Gulf War of 1991.

COUNTRY OF ORIGIN: United Kingdom	
CREW: 4	
WEIGHT: 137,500 lb (62,500 kg)	
DIMENSIONS: length 35 ft 4 in (11.55 m); width 10 ft 8 in (3.52 m); height 7 ft 5 in (2.49 m)	
RANGE: 250 miles (400 km)	
ARMOR: classified	
ARMAMENT: one 4.72 in (120 mm) gun; two 0.3 in (7.62 mm) machine guns; two smoke rocket dischargers	
POWERPLANT: one liquid-cooled diesel engine developing 1200 hp (895 kW)	
PERFORMANCE: maximum road speed 35.6 mph (57 km/h); fording 3 ft 4 in (1 m); vertical obstacle 2 ft 10 in (0.9 m); trench 9 ft 2 in (2.8 m)	

The Challenger 2 is arguably the best main battle tank in the world, and is a worthy successor to the problematical Challenger 1.

The Challenger 2 is the current main battle tank of the British Army. The hull is similar to the Challenger 1, as is the powerpack, but the turret has been redesigned to fit updated armament. In many ways it is a totally new tank.

Reducing visible detection

The first production versions appeared in mid-1994, boasting a carbon dioxide laser rangefinder, thermal imaging and fully computerized fire-control systems, giving a high first-round hit probability. In addition, turret traverse is all electric and the gun is fully stabilized. It can also be fitted with the Battlefield Information Control System in future years, for even greater combat capability. Stealth is designed into the tank's construction to reduce the probability of detection on the battlefield by visual, electronic and thermal means. All explosive material is stowed below the turret ring in armored charge bins and a Nuclear, Biological and Chemical (NBC) filtration system provides collective protection against ingress and maintains a positive vehicle internal pressure. Nearly 400 were ordered by the British Army, with 18 being exported to Oman.

The Challenger 2 closely resembles its predecessor, Challenger 1, but it is essentially a new tank, with 150 improvements having been made to the hull alone.

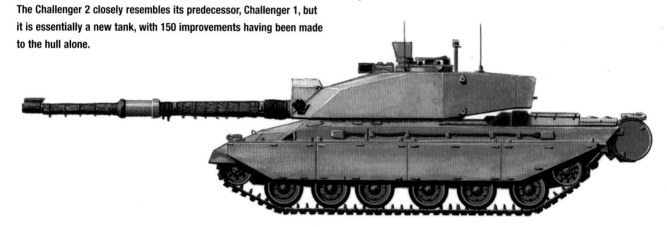

Glossary

AA Anti-Aircraft.

AAMG Anti-Aircraft Machine Gun, usually mounted on top of the turret of armored vehicles.

AAV Assault Amphibian Vehicle. US term for armored tracked amphibians used by Marine Corps, formerly called Landing Vehicle Tracked or LVT.

AAVC Assault Amphibian Vehicle, Command. AAV with additional communications fit for unit commanders.

ACP Armored Command Post. Armored vehicle with extra communications gear used by commanders in the field.

AFD Automatic Feeding Device. System for feeding ammunition from magazine into breech mechanically.

AFV Armored Fighting Vehicle. Generic term for military vehicles with armor protection and armament.

AP Armor Piercing. Ammunition designed to penetrate and destroy armored targets. Term usually reserved for solid shot fired at high velocity.

APC Armored Personnel Carrier. APCs, usually armed with machine guns, generally transport infantry to the battle before the troops dismount to fight on their own.

ballistics The science of studying projectiles and their paths. Ballistics can be "interior" (inside the gun), "exterior" (in-flight), or "terminal" (at the point of impact).

ditched A tank is ditched when the trench it is being driven across is too wide or the ground beneath is too soft or waterlogged to allow the tracks to grip.

DP Dual-purpose. When a weapon is intended for more than one job, or a round of ammunition has more than one effect, it is said to be dual-purpose.

FCS Fire Control System. Computers, laser rangefinders, optical and thermal sights and gunlaying equipment designed to enable a fighting vehicle to engage the enemy accurately.

fording Depth of water which a military vehicle can wade through without flooding engine. Usually quoted as without preparation and with preparation.

FV Fighting Vehicle. Term used by the British Army to identify vehicles accepted for service. For example the FV432 was Britain's standard APC for nearly 30 years.

GPMG General-Purpose Machine Gun. MG used as both infantry LMG and for sustained fire. Variants adapted as coaxial guns for tanks and as anti-aircraft guns on many different kinds of armored vehicle.

gradient Degree of slope up which a tank can travel.

grenades Originally hand-thrown high-explosive and fragmentation bombs, but also applied to weapons delivered by grenade launchers. Tanks usually have some kind of grenade-launching system to deliver smoke grenades.

HE High Explosive.

HEAP High Explosive Anti-Personnel. Dual-purpose HE round that destroys by a combination of blast and anti-personnel effects.

HEAT High Explosive Anti Tank. Tank round or guided missile with shaped-charge warhead designed to burn through the thickest of armor.

HESH High Explosive Squash Head. British term for HEP.

LRV Light Recovery Vehicle.

MG Machine gun.

muzzle brake Device attached to the gun muzzle to reduce recoil force without seriously limiting muzzle velocity.

muzzle velocity Speed of projectile as it leaves the muzzle. Air friction means velocity drops rapidly once in flight.

RP Rocket propelled. Applied to tank ammunition, artillery rounds and antitank grenades.

RPG Rocket Propelled Grenade Launcher. Soviet-made infantry antitank weapons.

running gear The transmission, suspension, wheels and tracks of a tank.

shell Hollow projectile normally fired from a rifled gun. Shell can have a number of fillings, including HE, submunitions, chemical and smoke.

shot Solid projectile, usually armor-piercing.

SMG Sub machine gun. Small fully automatic weapon often carried as personal arm by armored crewmen.

trajectory The curved path of a projectile through the air.

transmission Means by which the power of the engine is converted to rotary movement of wheels or tracks. Transmission can be hydraulic mechanical or electrical.

traverse The ability of a gun or turret to swing away from the centerline of a vehicle. A fully rotating turret has a traverse of 360 degrees.

tread Distance between the centerlines of a vehicle's tracks or wheels.

trench Field fortification that the tank was developed to deal with. Expressed as a distance in feet or meters in a tank's specification, trench indicates the largest gap a tank can cross without being ditched.

turret Revolving armored box mounting a gun. Usually accommodates commander and other crew.

turret ring Ring in the hull on which the turret rides supported by bearings. The size of the turret ring affects the size of the gun that can be fitted: the larger the ring, the larger the gun.

TRV Tank Recovery Vehicle

unditching beam Heavy wooden beam carried on early tanks. Mounted transversely across the tracks, it was used to gain extra grip when the tank was bogged down.

VDU Visual Display Unit.

velocity The speed of a projectile at any point along its trajectory, usually measured in feet per second or meters per second.

vertical volute spring Suspension with road wheels mounted to a bogie in pairs on arms, pivoting against a vertically mounted volute spring, it is protected from damage by the bogie frame.

WAM Wide Area Munitions. New area effect munitions designed to spread intelligent submunitions over a wide area.

whippet WWI term originally describing the first medium tanks, later to describe any light tank.

zippo track Vietnam slang for an M113 APC converted to a mechanized flame-thrower under the designation M132A2.

For More Information

American Armored Foundation Tank Museum
3401 U.S. Highway 29B
Danville, VA 24540
(434) 836-5323
Web site: http://www. aaftankmuseum.com/index.html
The mission of the tank museum is to collect, restore, preserve, and exhibit a significant part of military tank and cavalry artifacts from all time periods and nations as is possible and to educate present and future generations to the service and sacrifices given by the men and women of the armed services.

The Army Historical Foundation
2425 Wilson Boulevard
Arlington, VA 22201
(800) 506-2672
Web site: http://www. armyhistory.org

The Army Historical Foundation was established in 1983 as a member-based, publicly supported, nonprofit organization dedicated to preserving the history and heritage of the American soldier. The foundation seeks to educate future Americans to fully appreciate the sacrifices that generations of American soldiers have made to safeguard the freedoms of this nation.

National Military History Center
P.O. Box 1
Auburn, IN 46706
(260) 927-9144
Web site: http://www. militaryhistorycenter.org
The National Military History Center (NMHC) spotlights the service and sacrifice of America's military through a variety of museum units and major galleries dedicated to America's military, World War I, World War II, Korea, Vietnam, the Cold War, and today's War on Terror. The WWII Victory Museum is presently the centerpiece of this center, with other museums coming in the future.

The National World War II Museum
945 Magazine Street
New Orleans, LA 70130
(504) 527-6012
Web site: http://www. ddaymuseum.org
Renowned historian, author, and educator, Dr. Stephen Ambrose founded the National World War II Museum Foundation in New Orleans in 1991. The museum,

which opened on June 6, 2000, is the only museum in the United States that addresses all of the amphibious invasions or "D-Days" of World War II, honoring the more than one million Americans who took part in this global conflict.

U.S. Army Center of Military History

Fort Lesley J. McNair
Washington, DC 20319-5058
Web site: http://www.history.army.mil
The Center of Military History (CMH) is responsible for the appropriate use of history throughout the United States Army. Traditionally, this mission has meant recording the official history of the army in both peace and war, while advising the army staff on historical matters.

U.S. Army Heritage and Education Center

950 Soldiers Drive
Carlisle, PA 17013-5021
(717) 245-3419
The U.S. Army Heritage and Education Center's Mission is to educate a broad audience on the heritage of the army by acquiring, preserving, and making available historical records, materials, and artifacts. The AHEC vision is to become the premier center for US Army heritage focused on research, education, and interpretation.

The U.S. Army Ordnance Museum Foundation, Inc.

P.O. Box 699
Aberdeen Proving Ground, MD 21005
(410) 272-3622
Web site: http://www.ordmusfound.org/index.htm
The museum displays artillery equipment including small arms, military vehicles, aircraft bombs, fire control equipment, and armored fighting vehicles that have passed through the Aberdeen Proving Ground for tactical evaluation from the end of World War I to the present.

Web Sites

Due to the changing nature of Internet links, Rosen Publishing has developed an online list of Web sites related to the subject of this book. This site is updated regularly. Please use this link to access this list:

http://www.rosenlinks.com/grw/tank

For Further Reading

Bishop, Chris. *The Encyclopedia of Tanks and Armored Fighting Vehicles: From WWI to the Present Day*. San Diego, CA: Thunder Bay Press, 2006.

Cooper, Belton Y. *Death Traps: The Survival of an American Armored Division in World War II*. New York, NY: Presidio Press, 2003.

DK Publishing. *World War II: The Definitive Visual History*. New York, NY: DK Publishing, 2009.

Foss, Christopher F. *Jane's Tank Recognition Guide*. New York, NY: HarperCollins, 2006.

Green, Michael, and James D. Brown. *M2/M3 Bradley at War*. St. Paul, MN: Zenith Press, 2007.

Green, Michael, and James D. Brown. *M4 Sherman at War*. St. Paul, MN: Zenith Press, 2007.

Green, Michael, and James D. Brown. *Tiger Tanks at War*. St. Paul, MN: Zenith Press, 2008.

Green, Michael, and Gladys Green. *Panzers at War*. St. Paul, MN: Zenith Press, 2005.

Green, Michael, and Greg Stewart. *M1 Abrams at War*. St. Paul, MN: Zenith Press, 2005.

Green, Michael, and Greg Stewart. *Modern U.S. Tanks and AFVs*. St. Paul, MN: Zenith Press, 2003.

Holmes, Richard. *World War II in Photographs*. London, England: Seven Oaks, 2008.

Keegan, John, ed. *Collins Atlas of World War II*. New York, NY: Collins, 2006.

Miller, David. *The Great Book of Tanks: The World's Most Important Tanks from WWI to the Present Day*. St. Paul, MN: Zenith Press, 2003.

A New Illustrated History of World War II: Rare and Unseen Photographs 1939–1945. Newton Abbot, England: David & Charles, 2005.

Stolley, Richard B. *Life: World War II: History's Greatest Conflict in Pictures*. New York, NY: Bulfinch, 2005.

Yeide, Harry. *The Tank Killers: A History of America's WWII Tank Destroyer Force*. Drexel Hill, PA: Casemate, 2005.

Index

About the Editor

Robert Jackson is the author of over eighty books on military, aviation, naval, and scientific subjects. He was defense and science correspondent for a major newspaper publishing group. His expertise has led to books covering major studies of all aspects of individual military campaigns and wars.